Action for social
justice in education

Action for social justice in education

Fairly different

Morwenna Griffiths

with Sharon Baillon, Ghazala Bhatti, Max Biddulph, Eulalee Brown, Deborah Chetcuti, Roy Corden, Rita Dobbins, Kenneth Dunkwu, Ian Gibbons, Maxine Greene, Betty Kennedy, Edwin Maxwell, Jennifer Maxwell, Syble Morgan, Jon Nixon, Prakash Ross, Anne Seller, Madge Spencer, Perry Taylor, Nada Trikić, Melanie Walker, Joseph Windle

Open University Press
Maidenhead · Philadelphia

Open University Press
McGraw-Hill Education
McGraw-Hill House
Shoppenhangers Road
Maidenhead
Berkshire
England
SL6 2QL

email: enquiries@openup.co.uk
world wide web: www.openup.co.uk

and

325 Chestnut Street
Philadelphia, PA 19106, USA

First published 2003

A catalogue record of this book is available from the British Library

ISBN 0 335 19901 1 (pb)   0 335 19902 X (hb)

Library of Congress Cataloging-in-Publication Data
CIP data applied for

Typeset by RefineCatch Limited, Bungay, Suffolk
Printed in Great Britain by Biddles Limited, www.biddles.co.uk

Contents

List of co-authors and contributors

Sharon Baillon is a cleaner at Nottingham Trent University. She was brought up in Worcestershire. She previously worked in a paintbrush factory, a mental hospital, a physically handicapped centre, as a home help and as a childminder.

Ghazala Bhatti lectures in the School of Education at the University of Reading. She was brought up in Pakistan and England in the 1960s and 1970s. She previously taught in primary and secondary schools in Manchester and Sheffield, and at the Open University. She has also been a Research Fellow at Oxford University.

Max Biddulph lectures in the Centre for the Study of Human Relations in the School of Education at Nottingham University. He was brought up in Derbyshire in the 1960s and 1970s. He previously taught in secondary schools in South Yorkshire and Derbyshire. He was one of the Nottingham Group for Social Justice who worked with me in developing the principles for social justice for schools. (See Chapter 10.)

Eulalee Brown is a social worker in Birmingham. She was brought up in Jamaica and Yorkshire in the 1960s and 1970s. She previously worked in a number of capacities for the Harambee Organisation in Birmingham.

Deborah Chetcuti lectures in the Faculty of Education in the University of Malta. She was brought up in Malta in the 1960s and 1970s. She previously taught in secondary schools and was an officer in MATSEC, the examinations board.

Roy Corden is Reader in Education at Nottingham Trent University. He was brought up in Staffordshire in the 1950s and 1960s. He previously taught in primary, middle and secondary schools in Staffordshire, and was a local authority coordinator for the National Oracy Project.

Rita Dobbins has recently retired from her post as a Research Assistant at Nottingham University. She was brought up in Nottinghamshire in the 1940s and 1950s. She previously worked in the civil service as an administrative officer.

Kenneth Dunkwu works as a researcher and trainer for the 'Build' organiza-tion in Nottingham. He was brought up in Nottingham in the 1970s and 1980s. He has also worked as a researcher and trainer, for Nottingham University and Nottingham Trent University. He is a Visiting Fellow at Nottingham Trent University.

Ian Gibbons is a senior lecturer in primary mathematics education at Nottingham Trent University. He was brought up in London in the 1950s and 1960s. He previously taught in primary schools in Nottinghamshire.

Maxine Greene is professor of philosophy and education and William F. Russell Professor in the Foundations of Education (emerita), Teachers College, Columbia University, where she is also founder of the Center for the Arts, Social Imagination, and Education. She is Philosopher-in-Residence at Lincoln Center Institute for the Arts in Education and is past president of the American Educational Research Association, the American Educational Studies Association and the Philosophy of Education Society. She was brought up in New York in the 1920s and 1930s.

Betty Kennedy has retired from full-time work. She was brought up in Nottinghamshire in the 1930s and 1940s. She previously worked as a comp-tometer operator and as a company secretary, as well as bringing up her family.

Edwin Maxwell is the managing director of EAM Building Group. He was brought up in Jamaica and Nottingham in the 1960s and 1970s. He was an electrician in Nottingham and on the North Sea oil field in the Shetlands, before setting up his own business. He is married to Jennifer Maxwell.

Jennifer Maxwell is a Programme Director for 'Common Purpose', in Nottingham. She was brought up in Jamaica and Nottingham in the 1960s and 1970s. She previously worked as a health visitor and as a university lecturer. She is married to Edwin Maxwell.

Syble Morgan has recently retired as head of a local authority nursery in Birmingham. She was brought up in Jamaica in the 1940s and 1950s and moved to England in her twenties when she was a nurse. As a member of the Harambee Organisation in Birmingham, she helped to found Marcus Garvey nursery in 1978, one of the first Black community nurseries in Britain. She was its first head. She was one of the Nottingham Group for Social Justice who worked with me in developing the principles for social justice for schools. (See Chapter 10.)

Jon Nixon is Head of the School of Education at the University of Sheffield. He was brought up in Yorkshire and what was then Westmorland in the 1950s and 1960s. He has previously held Chairs at Canterbury Christ Church University College and the University of Stirling.

Prakash Ross is the Senior Advisor for the Ethnic Minority Achievement Service in Sheffield. He was brought up in London in the 1950s and 1960s. He previously taught in secondary schools in London (ILEA), Northamptonshire, Leicester and Nottingham. He has been an advisor in several Local Authorities. He was one of the Nottingham Group for Social Justice who worked with me in developing the principles for social justice for schools. (See Chapter 10.)

Anne Seller has recently retired from the University of Kent at Canterbury, where she lectured in philosophy and helped to found one of the earliest British MAs in women's studies. She was brought up in Bedfordshire in the 1940s and 1950s.

Madge Spencer is a successful potter and story teller. She was brought up in Jamaica in the 1940s and 1950s, and moved to England in her twenties. She has taught pottery in Jamaica and in England.

Perry Taylor is a reception and security officer in the Faculty of Education at Nottingham Trent University. He was brought up in Nottingham in the 1960s and 1970s. He previously worked as a dyer, a miner and a driving instructor.

Nada Trikić is head of Bramcote Hills Comprehensive in Nottingham. She was brought up in Chester in the 1950s and 1960s. She previously taught in secondary schools in Chester, Ashfield and Nottingham. She was one of the Nottingham Group for Social Justice who worked with me in developing the principles for social justice for schools. (See Chapter 10.)

Melanie Walker is a senior lecturer in education at Sheffield University. She was brought up in Durban, South Africa, in the 1950s and 1960s. She previously worked at the University of the Western Cape, Glasgow University and the University of the West of England, Bristol.

Joseph Windle is the administrator of the Centre for Research and Development in Education at Nottingham Trent University. He was brought up in Lincolnshire in the 1970s and 1980s. He previously worked in the retail sector.

Acknowledgements

This book has been over six years in the making. Over that time I have built up a debt of gratitude to many people. I can only thank some of them here. Others, many others, have contributed to its making and I am sorry that I cannot mention you all.

Thank you to Barbara Cross for introducing me to Betty Kennedy's story. And to Aisha and Calla, who patiently let me interview them a second time, when the tape had failed to record the first time. I am grateful to whoever it was in the two British Educational Research Association Day Seminars on social justice who came up with the slogan: 'social justice is a verb'. I am also indebted to the participants in both seminars for providing so much food for thought – even though it also provided Kenneth Dunkwu and me with far more work than we had thought we were taking on in producing the review!

I have been lucky to be working in the Faculty of Education at Nottingham Trent all the time I have been working on this book. It has provided a conducive atmosphere for working on the ideas in it. Graham Impey and Philip Garner, especially, have helped in working out ideas about partnership. Other colleagues, including the research students' methodology course members, have helped with working out puzzles around 'what is a theory?' I was also helped in this by participants at the British Philosophy of Education Annual Conference (2000) in Oxford, both in the workshop and at the bar afterwards. The social justice research cluster at Nottingham Trent, in its many incarnations, has been a home for ideas worked out in many meetings on campus and in pubs – if 'meetings' is the right word for occasions so full of laughter. They are, especially, Tony Cotton, Philip Garner, Sylvia McNamara, Connie Marsh, Dina Poursanidou and Sue Wallace. Colleagues in the Education Research Unit will also know how much I owe them for continuing companionship, support, laughter and a steady commitment to making theory and research useful and accountable: Elsie Blackwell, Dina Poursanidou, Joseph Windle and Karen Chantrey Wood.

The book demonstrates my continuing debt to the original 1995–6 Nottingham Social Justice group: Beryl Bennett, Max Biddulph, Carolyn Goddard, June Hunter, David Martin, Syble Morgan, Carol Price, Prakash Ross, Jacky Smith and Nada Trikić. Many of its members have contributed to this book. Their generosity, wisdom and passion for justice continue to inspire and challenge me.

I have been fortunate to find national and international networks that combine humanity and intellectual challenge, in a way that characterizes the best conditions for learning. The biennial Herstmonceux Castle conferences on Self-study of Teacher Education Practices is one such. Sandra Weber, who I met there, visited our university at a critical time for me in working out the shape of this book, and was very helpful. The 'Doing Citizenship' group, Jean Barr, Jon Nixon and Melanie Walker, has provided endless stimulation and sources of 'really useful' theory for justice in the intervening years. It was planned on a trip up the Mississippi during AERA in New Orleans, but survived 're-entry' into ordinary university life and has lasted years. This book bears the imprint of that group, as they will know.

Two chapters started life as joint papers: Chapter 5 with Debbie Chetcuti and Chapter 9 with Maxine Greene. Both these were distance collaborations, mostly by e-mail in one case and mostly by an uncertain snail mail in the other. Both, in different ways, helped to sustain me and keep me focused on the matter in hand, despite all the inspection and funding pressures that assail anyone working in Faculties of Education in universities in Britain over the past few years.

Most especially, I want to thank the 22 people who helped to write this book by contributing their stories and by responding to my chapters. Thank you to all of them. I know that they are all busy people who have responded to my requests with patience, courtesy, humour and humanity. Kenneth managed to read and respond to the book in a ridiculously short space of time. The process of obtaining the stories included some particularly happy times. I remember with pleasure: Madge's and Rita's gardens; Eddie and Jennifer's memorable dinner; companionable conversations with Syble in all kinds of corners; laughs, scams and parties with those from NTU; discussing perspectives on Arendt with Maxine, with our fingers on the text – and, extraordinarily, she wondered why I preferred this to sightseeing in New York!

Finally, as he knows, Peter, without whom I could not have done it.

Thanks are due to: the Philosophy of Education society for paying for me to go to New York, to discuss the article with Maxine Greene; to Nottingham Trent University for supporting my attendance at conferences in Canada, England, Scotland, Slovenia and the USA and for paying for transcription by Betty 'Gold-dust' Smith.

Earlier versions of articles reworked in this book are to be found in:

Chetcuti, D. and Griffiths, M. (2002) The implications for student self-esteem of ordinary differences in different schools: the cases of Malta and England. *British Educational Research Journal*, **28**(4), 529–49.

Dunkwu, K. and Griffiths, M. (2001) *Approaching Social Justice in Education: Theoretical Frameworks for Practical Purposes*. London: BERA (http://www.bera.ac.uk).

Greene, M. and Griffiths, M. (2002) Feminism, philosophy and education: imagining public spaces. In N. Blake, P. Smeyers, R. Smith and P. Standish (eds) *The Blackwell Guide to the Philosophy of Education*. Oxford: Blackwell.

Griffiths, M. (1993) Self-identity and self-esteem: achieving equality in education. *Oxford Review of Education*, **19**(3), 301–17.

Griffiths, M. (1999) Playing at/as being authentic. In J. Swift (ed.) *Art Education Discourses: Leaf and Seed*. Birmingham: ARTicle Press.

Griffiths, M. (2000) Collaboration and partnership in question: knowledge, politics and practice. *Journal of Education Policy (Philosophical Perspectives on Education Policy)*, **15**(4), 383–95.

Griffiths, M. (2001) Social justice for education: what kind of theory is needed? *School Field, Justice in/and Education*, **12**(1/2), 25–41.

Griffiths, M. (2002) 'Nothing grand': small tales and working for social justice. In J. Loughran and T. Russell (eds) *Reframing Teacher Education Practices: Exploring Meaning through Self-study*. London: Falmer Press.

Griffiths, M. and Haw, K. with Nehaul, K., Watling, R., Khan, S., Mian, S., Munir, F. and Siddiqui, A. (1996) *Equality and Quality for Asian Schoolchildren*. Nottingham: University of Nottingham.

Introduction

And our teachers report that he never interfered with their education.
Was he free? Was he happy? The question is absurd:
Had anything been wrong, we should certainly have heard.

(W. H. Auden, *The Unknown Citizen*)

A fair bit of difference

This book is about action for social justice, particularly in educational contexts. It pays attention to the real complexity of the issues, while at the same time suggesting strategies and principles for action, and illustrating these with real examples of how to implement them. It addresses the tensions between wanting equality at the same time as acknowledging difference: getting a fair deal for all. Many different people have contributed to the book, so it has been enriched by their different voices and points of view.

Who is the book written for?
And how might they read it?

The book is written for those in the thick of it – like me! They are teachers, headteachers, school governors, policy makers, educational researchers, teacher educators, university tutors and university administrators – many of whom share my strong feelings about getting social justice in education. It is also intended for the kinds of people who helped me to write it by adding their voices. They are introduced in the next section.

Different audiences have different interests, reading habits and motivations. So the book has been purposely written so that it need not be read from the beginning to the end. Some readers will want to pick out the stories (in Part 1). These are individual accounts of experiences of education. Other readers may wish to turn first to the 'Getting Real' cases (in Part 2). These contain practical examples of how the ideas can be put into practice. Some readers will be more interested in overarching theoretical arguments (such as: what is social justice?), while others will be more interested in particular areas (such as self-esteem). As far as possible, I have written each chapter so that it is free-standing, and can be read without reference to the others – and at the same time so as to make sure that the book is a coherent whole. (Inevitably, there is some repetition between chapters.) Part 1 has a linear logic. The argument builds up and is brought together in Chapter 4. However, Chapters 5–9 form a cycle (explained at the end of Chapter 4), so none of these chapters is the logical place to begin. Moreover, there is no reason to read Part 1 before Part 2. Chapter 10 contains a short section, 'The take home message', which summarizes the main lessons of the book. However, the chapter does not 'conclude'. Instead it leaves the discussion open, since getting social justice is always 'unfinished business', to be found in the actions taken towards it, rather than in any imagined Utopia.

Co-authors: who, what, how?

Twenty-two people helped to write this book by contributing their stories and by responding to my chapters. Between them, they have contributed nearly a third of the book, saving me from writing a book that advocated taking multiple perspectives through listening and conversation – and them doing it all by myself, from just one perspective. Some of the contributors have given an insight into what, for them, were the pains and pleasures, prizes and pitfalls of their education. Others have helped me, by providing responses to chapters, so as to keep the theorizing open rather than closed, unfinished rather than concluded. As the contributions came in, I found I was making more and more space for them, so interesting were they.

I want to say something about who the contributors are and how their contributions were made. In particular, I want to be clear about why I include them as contributors – co-authors – rather than as research subjects.

In order to find the contributors, I drew on personal and professional encounters of my everyday life. Some people (those in Part 1) told me stories of their education. These stories were mostly told as part of a taped conversation. Three were written. Inevitably the tapes were much too long to be included verbatim – nor had that ever been the intention. So I selected excerpts from the transcripts of our conversations. My selection was given to the person concerned, giving them full control to change anything at all – or everything – about what parts were selected and what was included. However, necessarily, I had a lot of influence here. In six cases, I asked if I could use conversations or writing that had been produced earlier for various reasons, explaining my purpose in this book and inviting them to change anything if they wanted. (One person changed nearly everything at this point.) In every other case, where I asked for a contribution specifically for this book, I invited the contributors to comment on my interests and my agenda, but they did not have to stick to that. In fact, each taped talk was as much a conversation as an interview or a dialogue. It is a feature of conversation that it can veer away from the agenda set by the first speaker, and need not return. So, what I taped was less a fact- or opinion-finding interview, more of a view-forming encounter.

Some (those in Part 2) responded to individual chapters. All of them are people whose views I respect, and whose perspectives overlap with mine: there is enough agreement and disagreement to make the encounter valuable. I invited each of them to 'answer back' to what I had said, without feeling that they had to 'reply' in the conventional academic sense. Chapter 5 has two respondents, rather than one. This chapter started life as a joint paper, with Deborah Chetcuti. Therefore, I asked her to respond to what I had made of our joint work, as well as asking someone else who had not been so closely involved. In every case, I have taken care not to respond to these responses within the book, in order to leave the conversation open. (The responses were all so interesting and thought-provoking that I am looking forward to continuing the dialogue elsewhere.)

The contributors were not a random sample of colleagues, friends and acquaintances. In choosing who to ask, I tried to make sure that I included perspectives from other socio-political positions, including those which are usually less well represented (see, for example, Mahoney and Zmroczek 1997). Each individual does not, of course, represent anyone other than themselves. To help ensure that nobody is taken to be *the* voice of any particular socio-political position, I have taken care to include more than one person in all the following categories: men; women; straight; gay/lesbian/bisexual; black; Asian; white; 'other minority ethnic'; middle-class background; working-class background; academically successful (that is, have a first degree); few educational accreditations (no university degree); youngish (twenties and thirties[1]); middling age (forties and fifties), oldish (sixties and above); teachers (including parents); parents (including teachers); British-born; British-settled; foreign.

Note

1 I included no school students. I interviewed some very articulate and perceptive young people in the last years of schooling. I was very interested in what they had to say about their motivation for learning and about their teachers. However, I was concerned that their stories might be identified, even if pseudonyms were used – and could be detrimental to them. So I made the decision not to include these contributions.

PART 1
Living with Difference

1 Justice and difference in education

Living with difference

The inquiry starts from the question: how is it possible to understand difference and diversity within a single humanity? This is a very difficult – but exhilarating – question. It is difficult to balance the knowledge that we are all the same in being human, with the knowledge that part of being human is, precisely, our unquenchable agency, our lovely creativity, our need and ability to make societies and communities: so that we are all – humanly – different. It matters how we understand this because we need to know how to work well with other people. That is, we need to know how to act fairly, intelligently and with humanity. And education is, inescapably and centrally, about working with other people.

It is always a temptation to simplify the issue by thinking that equality is sameness, and that our equal humanity means that everyone is the same. An alternative move, also tempting, is to reduce all difference to Otherness (other from whatever is dominant), or to simple categories of political identity (gender, race, sexuality and so on). I think these moves are tempting because alternatives are complex and difficult to grasp. Any alternative has to encompass: (a) individual differences of personality and temperament; (b) differences of social identification; and (c) differences of social positioning. And they have to do that without falling into stereotyping and, its reverse side, liberal angst. In Nancy Fraser's words (1997: 187):

> There is no going back to the old equality/difference debate in the sense of an exclusive focus on any single axis of difference. The shift from 'gender difference' to 'differences among women' to 'multiple intersecting differences' remains an unsurpassable gain, but this does not mean we should simply forget the old debate. Rather we now need to construct a new equality/difference debate.

And, I would add, the debate needs to include ineradicable individual differences too.

We live in a diverse society – a society made rich by its diversity. At last, this is becoming widely recognized. There have been real gains in the past few decades in how educational institutions approach issues of diversity. Oddly, however, there are still those who try to ignore it, so much do they yearn after more uniformity. Now, you might think that it is impossible to imagine a society with no diversity (one sex, one class, one ethnic background, uniform abilities, one religion). This sounds obviously wrong. I wish everyone thought so. However, the imaginations of so many leaders of our society – the policy makers and other influential people – seem to be fixed, stuck even, in a simplistic view of the world, in which people are very much less diverse than the rest of us know them to be. If there is diversity, it is mentioned in simplistic terms, apparently for fear of offending 'public opinion'.

It is instructive to examine current official pronouncements from the Department for Education and Skills. They mention the issues of difference only in terms of problems to be solved, rather than resources on which to draw. A major speech, 'Transforming secondary education', was made by the Secretary of State, Estelle Morris, in March 2002. She talked of 'multiple disadvantages', 'areas of high deprivation' and relatively low achievement by boys in English, and by Black boys at GCSE. She then went on to propose a strategy in terms of specialist schools, better quality teaching and targeting individual pupils. The strategy seems to be directed at getting every student to become closer to an ideal student – an ideal as much like the imaginary 'white-male-middleclass-heterosexual-ablebodied' as possible. In August 2002, Morris gave another speech, 'Excellence across sectors', in which she referred to the traditional elite sector as the hallmark of excellence (Morris 2002b):

> In opposing the way in which our top education institutions were too often the reserves of the well off, [the Labour party] made the mistake of not just opposing the achievement of privilege, but also the achievement of excellence itself.

Similarly, consider the following, reported in the *Times Higher Education Supplement*, which attracted criticism, rather than outrage or demands for resignation (Tysome 2002):

> Research commissioned by the Council for Industry and Higher Education shows a significant earnings divide between graduates from lower and those from higher social groups, irrespective of which institution they attended ... Richard Brown, CIHE chief executive, ... said: 'At the moment, the thinking seems to be that if you can recruit the unwashed, then all will be fine. But social skills still count for an

awful lot. These skills are often bred into you if you come from a certain social class, but they are not if you were born on the wrong side of the tracks. Institutions need to think about how individuals' life skills can be developed where they are absent as a result of upbringing.'

In fact, society is becoming more diverse, rather than less. There is an irreducible diversity in any society because gender, class and a range of (dis)-abilities and sexualities are always there. Some areas of the UK – and some areas of the world – still appear startlingly monocultural with respect to ethnicity and religion. Many of them appear to be trying to wish away the existence of social class. But social class remains, even if it is more fragmented than it was in the nineteenth century. And all areas of the world are becoming more multicultural in relation to ethnicity and religion too. Migration is nothing new, and today's may indeed be smaller in scale than previous global movements of people: witness the appropriation of Australia, New Zealand and much of the Americas by migrants. However, migration is now more likely to be from poorer to richer countries, and so it results in new patterns of multicultural society in the West (Castles and Miller 1998). On an experiential level, consider how everyday life in the educational institutions of any modern city includes encounters with: girls and boys; men and women who may be Muslim, Christian, Hindu, Jewish, and secular versions of each of these; rich and poor; black, white and the rainbow of ascribed colours in between, including children of 'mixed race'; gay, straight and undecided; migrant, indigenous, recently settled, migrant for generations; rural, town-dwelling and metropolitan. Consider the possible permutations and combinations of all of these. Then add in an array of different physical and mental abilities and disabilities.

It is hardly surprising that there are a range of answers to questions about the uses of education, the pleasures and pains of learning and teaching, the glittering prizes and the booby traps to be found as the result of an engagement with the education system and the kinds of self-perceptions that are developed in that engagement. The system as it is now (in all its variety) works differently for different people. Partly this is a matter of individuality – think of the young boy, Peter Porter, discovering poetry in his primary school in suburban Queensland, Australia, and growing up to become one of the best known modern poets in Britain.[1] But it is also a matter of systematic – and unfair – difference of social and political position. Bourdieu (1977: 493) put it elegantly:

> The action of the school, whose effect is unequal among children from different classes, and whose success varies considerably among those upon whom it has an effect, tends to reinforce and to consecrate by its sanctions the initial inequalities.

Consider the examples of some of those combinations and permutations to be found in the descriptions of educational experience in the narratives of this chapter and the following ones. They have been interwoven with my own writing throughout Part 1 of the book. The next section tells some of Ian Gibbons's story, first as a pupil and then as a teacher. All the narratives make it abundantly clear that education can produce flourishing, but also that it can produce felt unfairness and actual injury to the well-being of both pupils and teachers. We can also see that for most people their encounters with the education system have probably included both good and bad. These narratives exemplify how diversity of perspective is a resource, which can be used to frame an understanding of how to get the best from our education system. By 'education system' I mean not only schools but also further and higher education establishments, and more informal institutions. By 'the best' I mean the best for *everyone*. It is also clear – and this is significant for all educators, and their policy makers – that there is not, and *could not be*, a single view of the purpose of education. A 'good education', judged by process and by outcome, is not the same for all sectors of society, nor for all the individuals in any one sector.

This book explores the following two questions of fairness and difference:

1 How should we best live with the lovely diversity of human beings?
2 How can education best benefit all individuals and also the society in which they live?

It does so with the intention of providing action for change for the better.

Ian Gibbons. Freedom to be successful

My background is being brought up in the street in which all the problem families were put. My Mum had camped out in the local county hall until we got a house and it just happened to be where all the big families were. I was one of five kids. Because I didn't pass my 11 plus, I went to secondary modern. I think I just kind of enjoyed being in the business of learning. I was painfully shy and quiet at school. Put me out amongst a group of lads playing football and I would kill anybody, but in school, I never spoke, was very embarrassed by everything.

I managed to survive secondary school, which I thought was particularly brutal. At secondary, there were no great pressures on us to achieve academically but there was a freedom to be successful. I can remember the head very clearly. I was very scared of him, but he was a great person who basically killed himself with overwork to try and help everybody. I got as many O-levels as anybody from the grammar school that year, which was quite a surprise, and went on to do A-levels.

I remember the careers teacher saying, 'What do you want to be when you leave school?'

'An archivist.'

She looked it up.

'No, you can't do that,' she said and slammed the book shut.

I just thought, 'Yes, we'll see.' I spent most of my time at university proving that it could be done and then trying to make it happen for other kids.

I got my deputy headship at 28. I have always been interested in kids and kids' things and being with kids and hearing what they have to say. The kids that we had were drawn from all over the county. It was the cheapest place to house people. A housing association took over part, which meant that a family tended to end up there because they couldn't pay their debts, because the family had split up, because of lost jobs. There were old traditional mining families that had been in the area for a long, long time who were distinctly anti-authority and it was just a mess. It was just a mess of broken families, relocated people.

The style of learning was crucial. Because if you gave them a piece of paper to colour in, they would sit there all day colouring in, no thought, no progress – and it managed them. So how do you get kids who don't want to engage, who don't want to be in the school really, to begin to think about stuff? That led, for instance, to the big idea of 'maths as pattern hunters' and to them 'being scientists'. Look at history, for example. History is about cause and effects. It is about personalities within sequences of events. So is it the events or is it the personalities? So we began to explore how is it that one person is able to dominate and make things happen in the way that millions of others have never been able to – cause and effect. One morning we fought the invasion of Britain by the Romans. I set up a computer program with messages coming through at set points and the kids responded by moving all the troops that they created and working at effective decision-making. Of course, we got clobbered because the Romans were better at it than us.

'OK, what do you learn from it?'

So all this was to do with: what are the big ideas?

The achievement was measured largely by the kids. Every alternate Friday afternoon we would fetch out all the things that they played with – all the things that they could do independently. I would go round each kid.

'Show me what you have done in the last two weeks. What have you really enjoyed? What didn't you like? Are you OK with where you've sat? What kind of things are you working on next?'

It was a struggle but kids were very clear about what they wanted from their work. I think I only ever had one kid who saw it as a game and refused to engage with it. Most of them were willing to see what they were working on and were genuinely trying to improve it.

I had one kid who dragged his mum off the street to come to the parents' evening. Of course, you only get four or five parents at the most. Now, his mum could neither read nor write.

'Come and have a look at my work. Look at this. This is what I am doing – it's good, isn't it?'

There were genuine conversations about what they were doing.

We found out from the careers lady at the secondary school that none of our kids had ever, in twenty years, stopped on beyond 14. Most of them didn't reach that point. They kind of wandered off from school. In the days when it wasn't that well controlled, our kids just didn't end up at school. We had three key teachers in the school – only three of us, three classes. We began to talk about how each of us was dealing with it and began to set up little projects about looking at each other's practice. We were beginning to influence children's willingness to move beyond the culture of the village to looking after themselves and looking beyond. We were absolutely delighted when we got our first kid who stopped on to do A-levels. Then one got to university. Absolutely delighted.

Questions of fairness and difference

How should we best live with the lovely diversity of human beings?

How should we best live with the lovely diversity of human beings? Diversity may be lovely, and it is also a resource. It is easy to agree with Hannah Arendt that:

> Wherever a civilisation succeeds in eliminating or reducing to a minimum the dark background of difference, it will end in complete petrification.
>
> (Arendt 1973: 302)

But too often diversity turns into stereotyping, hierarchies and the harmful formation of exclusive in-groups. As many feminists have pointed out, the self-proclaimed rationality of man depends on there being a 'residue' of irrationality among women, and other Others (e.g. Hughes 1988; Whitford 1991). A dynamic tension needs to play between the tendencies to fixity and fluidity. Christine Battersby (1998) helpfully uses the metaphor of a wave to describe form within fluidity. This book explores how to create and sustain such fluidity at the same time as acknowledging existing forms, within an educational context.

How can education best benefit all individuals and also society?

How can education best benefit all individuals and also, and at the same time, the society that they live in? This is a question of what to do in educational contexts so that the good of all does not depend on the ill of some. It is also a question of what to do so that the good of any individual (or small group of individuals) is not inimical to the good of everyone else. The question relates to individuals, not to types, though always remembering that they are individuals in relation to other people, that they are marked by their social and economic context. This is a question that is relevant in all contexts, from the smallest classroom or tutorial room to the schools and universities in which they function. (Think, for instance, of what to do about the special educational needs of one or two children within a classroom or, at a different level of generality, think of the admission policies of universities in relation to social class or gender.) The question is one that will not go away, because any answers must be provisional, given the mutual dependence of the development of both selves and structures.

Jennifer Maxwell. I was really angry

I came to Nottingham when I was seven, I suppose. They put me into Shelton Street Junior School and that was pretty awful. I thought it was a prison. This old Victorian building was down in St Ann's on Shelton Street and it was all brick walls. You actually went through an iron gate. The playground was just concrete. It was dusty. It was dirty. There was no greenery. It was damp; it was dank; it was dull. It was foggy. Lots of chimney smoke because of the type of area it was. I thought it was awful. It was like being in prison. The worst part was coming from Jamaica and having this thick Jamaican accent, but thinking that I was quite bright – but here the teachers and the children treated me as if I was quite stupid.

The children played strange games and they were pretty rough. They pushed each other and they kept taking the mickey out of me, calling me names. In the end I did get a friend, Deborah, and Deborah and I stayed friends right up until the end of junior school. Deborah befriended me and started defending me – she beat the others up. That was why they stopped picking on me because once I became Deborah's friend – nobody messed with Deborah.

In my final year I was in the same class as Deborah and that was the class they were prepping to do the 11 plus. I remember one day the headmaster came in the classroom and just pointed at a group of us, called out our names and, interestingly enough, it was all the black kids. I was separated from Deborah and told I was going to be in a different class. I can remember crying and saying I didn't want to leave Deborah because we always sat next to each other, did our work together and in a way it was like a competition between us to do things right. But it wasn't hostile. We just did it as a fun thing.

This class that they put me in I stayed in it for a few months and then I was really angry – very, very angry – with this teacher because I wanted to go back to Deborah and I wanted to do real work, proper work. She wanted us to pretend we were animals. One of these animals was being a snake. To be a snake you had to lie on the floor and you had to slither. I refused to go on the floor because I would dirty my clothes and I knew my mum would be really annoyed. I would probably get another beating and I refused. She tried to get me to go down on the floor so I kicked her and then I bit her. She went to get the headteacher and I had to go and see him in his office. He asked me why I was being so naughty.

'It is not like you Jennifer, you don't normally behave like this. I expect it of the other children, but not you.'

'I don't like it in there. I want to go back to my proper class. I want to be with Deborah and I want to do proper work,' I said. So he took me out and put me back in with Deborah.

My father went and bought a load of 11 plus papers and I was doing them at home with him as well. He was a bus driver for Nottingham City Transport and at the time my mum was working in Players factory. My dad did believe in education and wanted me to go to the grammar school. But my parents, with all their good intentions, they didn't know how the system worked. They didn't understand it, and not only that, I thought they were too respectful of it. When they went to the city council to get me a bus pass when I started at Manvers Pierrepont, this man said he couldn't find my record. He came back and said, 'She shouldn't be in that school. According to our records she passed the 11 plus. She should have been offered a place. Why wasn't she offered a place? Let me investigate this.' Then he came back and gave them some story and they never pushed it. I came out with four O-levels, at that time not enough to do A-levels.

Later, working as a health visitor, I had an argument in the office one day with one of my colleagues about 'Why on earth we had health visitors' and 'Why should we be interfering in people's lives?' and 'Basically isn't health visiting all about us telling people what to do because the powers that be want them to behave in a certain way?' I didn't have all the theories. I didn't have all the concepts. We had this massive argument and one of my colleagues was doing an OU degree and it sounded interesting. So I thought, 'Right! Maybe that will help me to sort this all out.' I rang up Nottingham University.

Oh, God! I couldn't believe it! I thought, 'What am I doing here at university? I'm so stupid!' And I just found it fascinating. I really enjoy it. I love being in the library. I love reading. I love talking about things. I love arguing about it. I love discussing it, debating it. I love finding out. I could sit in the library and just read. It was a great big world opened out and it started to help me to make sense of things. And now I have a PhD!

Why the questions matter: a question of justice?

The twin questions of diversity and benefit are urgent. They deal with perennial problems but they are, nevertheless, pressing. It is clear that there are great injustices that cry out to be put right, but that have remained intractable across the globe. For instance, research shows that in Britain, as in every other developed country, the expansion of higher education (and so a much better chance to earn more) has continued to benefit the middle classes disproportionately. In the past half-century, the chances of a British child from a working-class family going into higher education have increased from about 2 to 16 per cent, but those for a middle-class family have increased from 10 to 50 per cent. Figures for France, Japan and the USA tell a similar story. About 20 per cent of American students from poor backgrounds attend private (that is, the best) higher education institutions, compared to nearly 50 per cent of those from the top income decile (Wolf 2002). Race and gender, like social class, also divide universities. Surveys show that many women and many black and Asian staff believe institutional racism exists in universities. There are clear pay differentials for staff, and both courses and universities are becoming racially segregated. The *Guardian* (18 April 2002) reports that complaints in the courts are rising.

A similar picture continues for schools. In 2000, two-thirds (66 per cent) of students from middle-class backgrounds achieved at least five GCSEs above a C grade, compared to only two-fifths (40 per cent) of working-class students. This picture is cross-cut by race: 50 per cent of white children achieved at least five GCSEs compared to 40 per cent of black children, 30 per cent of Pakistani children and 60 per cent of Indian and other Asian children. Far more boys than girls are excluded from school (84 per cent of children excluded) and, of those, black Caribbean boys are almost four times as likely to be excluded as white boys (Office of National Statistics 2002). Schools in the inner cities are much more likely to have fewer resources even though their pupils are more likely to be faced with financial problems in their everyday lives. Nick Davies (1999) convincingly reviewed evidence that deprivation is the most powerful influence on a school's performance. Enora Brown's (2001) comparison of two schools in Chicago shows that this is not just a British disgrace.

Individual stories put the systematic research into context. Some of these are told in the stories woven into this chapter, and through the rest of Part 1. The experiences are not monolithic accounts of injustice or how to mitigate it. They show the complexities of what is felt as injustice and its mitigation. They also give some idea of the many ways in which large-scale, systematic injustice is constructed out of particular differences – and, equally, how some people can find ways to deal with it. These stories were chosen to give a range of diverse points of view, but they are also in one sense very ordinary: they are drawn from my own personal circle of acquaintance. They were certainly not selected out of some larger sample of stories. (See the Introduction for more details of how they were collected.)

I have stated that all of this – the statistical evidence, the stories – is a matter of justice. That is, it is a matter of what seems to be fair to the individuals concerned, and in the judgement of those of us who hear the stories. We might say that knowing what is fair or just needs no more than this. That is, it might be concluded that no theory is needed. But that conclusion would be wrong. A theory is needed to go on from that intuition, and to see how far these cases are similar and how far they are different. But it is important that the argument is seen to go in this direction. It does not start from an assumption of what social justice is (or, for that matter from any particular theory of social justice) and make these cases fit the definition. However, equally, it does not end with intuition. I say a lot more about theorizing 'social justice' in Chapter 3. For now, I just summarize what I have written elsewhere in various publications.

Very briefly then, I take a concern for 'social justice' to be the good of the community that respects – depends on – the good of the individuals within it, and the various sectors of society to which they belong. (In other words, the questions that are raised above concerning difference and diversity *are* questions of social justice.) It is a dynamic state of affairs that is never achieved once and for all. So we are all, individually and collectively, required to exercise constant vigilance, as we hold to a concern for individuals at the same time as focusing on broader issues of race, gender, sexuality, (dis)ability, religion, ethnicity, nationality, social class and any and all other differences that are systematically divisive in the society.

Madge Spencer. I was determined

I wanted to learn. I didn't know what the hell I wanted – I just knew I wanted to do something – like any child's eager mind to find things out.

This is what happened after I left school. I was oh, 22, 23. I was determined because I had a baby now, no support, on my own. I had done odd little jobs. So when my uncle gave me the offer to learn potting at the art college in Kingston, my God! I was determined to grasp it with two hands. Do the day, and then in the afternoon go and practise on the potter's wheel to make quick things, to make ashtrays and little pigs and little trinkets. As soon as I could finish them, my uncle was able to sell them in a tourists' market to finance my upkeep. Work! Work? Hah! I was at college, nine o'clock in the morning, and I left at ten to twelve at night to catch the last bus home. But I was young and fit and I just had this goal in mind. I did the two-year course, did all the other things during the day and in the evening I did that and I worked. I worked!

Then I met John Rivers who was a teacher. When we married, and went to England, I potted, I potted, as hard as I could for my contribution to my upkeep. We used to sell the pots, you see.

I started reading. I just stayed at home and work, work, work until I thought No, there must be more to life than this. So I took myself off to college and then

I was doing *Henry V*! I enrolled at Ilkeston College and did my O-level English literature and English language. I was, oh, 28 or 29. I put myself back to school because I was determined. I read the plays through and I had another friend at work to read together with. We did it together and enjoyed it. But my husband was one of those men who thinks that as a woman I should not be educated. He did not help. I failed but I took it again. I can't remember if I passed it the second time or the third time but I was determined. I kept going back until I passed. On my own, I passed. And now I am 60 years old and I am doing my A-level. The boys are off and I am settled. This is the new house. Now that I am here and I am comfortable and I am happy, I just want to prolong my education so that I read and read and read and it is my friend, it is my company, it is my teacher, it is my everything.

I teach potting to ages three to 15. I take the potter's wheel in and not many schools have a potter's wheel. They might have a bit of clay that they roll and twist into some little form. They might have got clay, have got a potter's wheel, have got everything, but they haven't got a teacher who really knows it. When you give a child an opportunity to make a pot from half past nine to ten o' clock and the child will look at you, holding their little pot and say, 'Can I take this home *now*?' Now, that must be something. They will be at school until three and they are so excited at having achieved this, they want to go home *now*.

I went into a comprehensive school, 15-year-olds, big young men. I have to look up when they are talking to me and their voices are down here. I did them a demonstration and they looked at me as if to say, 'Oh, God! What has she got to teach us?'

I ignored them because I knew very soon I would have them eating out of my hand. So I just smiled knowingly. I got my potter's wheel and they looked me up and down. I got my clay and they looked me up and down. I sat down and they looked around. Then I started to talk.

'This is the clay and it is wet. It has to be a certain condition before it is used for making the pot on the wheel. At home I have a kick wheel, but I prefer the electric one because it is easier and I can travel around with it. You put the clay on the wheel. This is what it looks like unaided.'

And it is wobble, wobble, wobble. And they say, 'Yes.'

'This is what you have to do in order to stop it from wobbling *before* you make the process of making a pot.'

I put my hand on the clay – wobble, wobble – and stop the wobble. Silence! They stopped what they were doing! They absolutely stopped.

'Ooooh!'

Because they had never seen it, you see. They may have seen it on TV but it is not the same.

I get that reaction every week. I know I have got them and I know I have got them eating out of my hand. Then I take the clay off again, let it wobble and they look, and I say, 'This is what it looks like.' Then when I open the clay: 'Ooooh!' I get that sort of reaction every time.

So I go through the stages: centring the clay, opening the clay, pushing the clay downward, pulling the clay upward and then bringing it up again higher. Then I show them how to get the shape and put the paint on. I probably throw three or four different shapes before they have a go. Well they can't wait. They can't wait to have a go.

These are all big 15 year olds. 'Madge! Oh please, Madge, can I make another one?' Then halfway through the session one beautiful young man said, 'Oh Madge, I wish you were my Mum!' Now isn't that a credit? Because I was talking to them, you see, and not only about pottery but talking about this and that, chatting, you know and just a relaxed atmosphere. I thought, 'That was good – for a 15-year-old boy to say that.'

Why the questions matter: a question of education?

Education is always and inescapably about individuals in a pedagogic relationship. It is personal. Here is an example from David, a teacher in inner-city London:

> My head is very kind, saying that I have a real way with challenging children. I think I do. I really like them best. This year I have Nya who has a wide repertoire of party tricks, including standing on tables and screaming and then slapping her teacher's face. We had it out the first day and I won. She is now my 'secretary' and we have given up all the old silly positive reinforcement nonsense she thinks is patronizing. We write down when she is naughty. She prefers this because it is only once a week or so and then she feels more normal. We also count the number of strands of hair she pulls out, another party trick. This has worked very well because she used to have nasty marks on her head and now has lovely hair with purple bits, my colour suggestion, woven in.

The when, from whom, how and what of learning remains unpredictable, mysterious and entwined with human relationships. There is no getting away from this. (Thank goodness!) As well as curiosity – which is unpredictable, though often cited as if it is uniform – there are fun, love, laughter, tears and obsessions. As Pádraig Hogan (1995) eloquently puts it, there are epiphanies of learning, which may come to an individual at a specific time. No wonder that learning escapes systems and foolproof methods. All this applies from age three to 63 and beyond; from nursery through tertiary education; through compulsory schools to Saturday schools to surfing the Internet. As the stories in this part of the book show, reasons for learning (or not) are always intensely personal. The same is true of teaching.

At the same time as being about human relationships, education is a science and a social science. It is dependent on hard facts about learning, bodies, growth. It is an important part of the state's economy. Indeed, it is a large state enterprise, and it is kept busy systematically sorting, classifying and stamping people in order to service the financial and political economy. (By using the term 'stamping' I invoke shades of Robert Burns: 'The rank is but the guinea stamp, / The man's the gold for a' that.') All this is just as inescapable as the pedagogic relationship, the subject of the previous paragraph.

So knowing what to do about social justice in education depends on ways of dealing with this continuing complexity, indeed tension. That is, it is necessary to use conceptual-theoretical frameworks that focus on the individual and also conceptual-theoretical frameworks that focus on society. As stated earlier, the starting point is: justice refers both to individual's personal circumstances and experience, and to systematic, institutional effects of different political and social positions, like race, class, gender and so on.

Joseph Windle. The most daunting thing

I'll start with primary school. The expectations were quite high but they were only bothered with the people they knew would pass the 11 plus. There didn't seem to be any support – though there was for the people that did well. I didn't think at the time I was treated unfairly, but I do now because I could see there wasn't the chance. I needed some sort of attention because I wasn't stupid but I wasn't totally bright and a star – although I was a good student.

And, of course, I didn't pass. I didn't expect to. I didn't think I could. We just got a letter one morning and the three schools that you could go to, with boxes next to them. They had ticked the one I was to go to.

I was the only boy from my primary school that went to that school. I lived further out than the others, so I had to go to a different secondary school. It was very hard because I literally lost all my friends.

Going to secondary school was so horrible to have to do on my own. It was the most daunting thing I have ever done. I can remember my first day when I stood in that secondary school in that yard with everyone. I was looking at everyone and they all knew each other. There were groups and I was stood there on my own. I thought, God! What the hell do I do now? It was horrible. Fortunately, someone came over to me. He was in a group and he came over to me. I must have been there for about 15 minutes and it was awful. I didn't know what to do. That 15 minutes seemed like three days. It was then that I knew that this school was going to be really tough. I needed to stick up for myself and I had never done that before.

It was so strange and it always felt so alien and horrible. I can remember when I met our form teacher. He was a PE teacher. He seemed all right to start with, but through the years at school, he only bothered about people who were good at PE.

If you weren't good at PE, if you weren't going to be entered for Sports Day, then you weren't really worth it. You weren't worth paying attention to. I remember when my dad died. I had been off for a week because of the funeral and everything. I went back and he said, 'Oh, can I see you?' And he was really nice to me. I thought, 'God! Does it take your dad to die to get some attention?'

The teachers never gave us any attention really, because they didn't seem to be bothered. They thought everyone was the same and were not interested in education. A lot of them weren't. To be fair, they weren't. They just messed about. The teachers couldn't control the people that were disruptive. All the classes seemed to be pretty much ridiculous and farcical. The teachers would say, 'This is your homework. You can do it if you like, it doesn't really make much difference.' I would do it but you would think, 'Why bother?'

I was lucky that I was friends with Wendy, not straight away, in about the third year. She was quite conscientious also. The English teacher I had at secondary school was really bad. In my final year English, Wendy and I would do all the work and we would sit there for weeks with nothing to do waiting for everyone to catch up. Wendy and I would sit there. We had nothing to do. We would chat to each other because he wouldn't give us anything to do. He was a terrible teacher. He couldn't control anybody. He would sit there reading a book and watching every-one making a row, throwing paper all over the place. He would say, 'Well I have got nothing for you to do until this lot have finished.' So I think that *did* hold me back.

Partly I don't regret going there because it has toughened me up. I can deal with situations. It was more about survival, that school. If I had not been there, people could quite easily walk all over me. I had to stick up for myself. I had to defend myself. But I am not confrontational. I think it's because there was so much confrontation in the school and that was something I hated. There were quite a lot of fights and that was horrible. I suppose that is something that I have learned: it is not something I want to be like. I wouldn't want to be like that.

I think I have got more confidence. That confidence, I think, has come from a college course I did after school. I hated college for the first four weeks. I really didn't like going. But as soon as we got settled in, I loved it and it was different because everyone wanted to be there. People were paying more attention to things and they took more of an interest in everything. I got a lot out of it. The people I was on the course with were really good so I enjoyed it. I was good at accounts. I got distinctions in it, which surprised me because I'd struggled at maths. I found it difficult at school and yet I enjoyed doing accounts because I could do it quite well. So I owe a lot to the college for that. It was a good experi-ence for me and I didn't want to leave.

It does feel very strange to think I have gone on to do a degree. It's unbeliev-able. I have struggled but then I have known where to have gone to get over that and to get help. We have had some awful tutors but then, we have had some really good ones as well. But it's the people that we were on the course with – it's Vicky and people like that. We knuckled down and got on with it on our own really.

Approaches to answering the questions

The approach that I have taken in answering the questions is 'practical philosophy' (as I call it). There is a continuing attention to practicalities and specificities while the theorizing continues, and a continuing attention to careful, rigorous, theory and reflection while presenting practicalities and specificities. Practical philosophy aims at being a philosophy that engages with the conditions of *all* people, women *and* men, poor *and* rich, Others *and* Us. It is a kind of philosophy that is interested in the empirical world as a way of grounding its conclusions in interaction between thinking and acting. At root, it is 'philosophy *as, with and for* . . .' rather than 'philosophy *about or applied to* . . .'; a kind of philosophy that acknowledges its own roots in the communities from which it sprang, and that then speaks with (at least) that community.[2] It links with practical concerns of those people: using practice in shaping the explicit formulations of theories and then in turn using those explicit formulations to see what might best be done. Knowledge is produced in relation to significant Others, rather than through them or for them. Theory is brought into question by the experience it questions and is then used to inform practical actions. Theoretically sophisticated concepts and arguments are used to frame interpretations of particular, real, messy, practical situations, as understood by the people involved in them.

My approach to understanding justice has risen out of a tradition of work that pays a lot of attention to voice and to personal experience. There is no doubt that such an approach has dangers and drawbacks, especially because without a continuing focus on power and structure, it has a tendency to relapse into the cosiness of apolitical individualism. When it does, more emphasis needs to be placed on social and political structures and relations. Over the years, my own work has relied on the critical use of autobiographies and anecdotes chosen to be from different social and political positions, e.g. those of gender, race, sexuality, social class and Special Educational Needs.

My approach to understanding justice also arose from paying attention to the social and political. This approach also has dangerous drawbacks. An over-emphasis in that direction leads to the opposite danger of over-generalization and abstraction. An approach that focuses primarily on large-scale power and structure can dangerously over-simplify the complexities of how particular agents may articulate the material constraints of their lives, and sometimes transform them. It is liable to reify identity. Further, it has been the source of bitter arguments within the politics of social justice, as various identity groups (identified by combinations of class, disability, gender, global position, race, religion and sexuality) have found themselves overlooked and silenced. Plainly, it is impractical to have a separate policy for each kind of injustice, for each strand. There are too many strands and anyway all of them change over time and context. Equally, a policy that does not recognize differences is falling into the same kind of trap as the single perspective that diversity is trying to get away from. Without a continuing focus on the intractable complexity of lives, large-scale explanations have a tendency to relapse into the comforts of certainty and of having explanations of everything.

This book is an experiment in combining both approaches. The structure of the book attempts to cover both individual and abstract approaches, without losing either. I want to take forward the equality/difference debate in such a way that it is of practical help, accountable to real lives, but at the same time theoretically robust. The framework I develop in Part 1 is explained in Chapter 4, and used to structure Part 2.

Notes

1   Peter Porter told this story during a professorial lecture at Nottingham Trent University in 2000.
2   I am grateful to Victoria Perselli for pointing out that 'as' is important here. It indicates that the philosopher is part of the community.

2   Whose education is it anyway?

Whose education?

Whose education is it? Is it owned by the government, which pays for much of it? Or by the students (or their parents), who pay individually? Some of the contributors to this book say they were robbed or cheated of an education, and that sounds as if their education was taken away from them. For many of them, this is about more than being cheated of formal equality of access – though some of the contributors to this book relate how even this minimal equality was lacking for them. A key issue raised by groups marked by their political and social positions (for example, of gender, race, social class, disability and sexuality) is the way a system of education can be used to benefit only a few. Exclusive or competitive systems of education can be damaging to whole sectors of society, or to large numbers of individuals within it.

Education costs a lot, but nevertheless it cannot be rightfully bought or owned. Like health, family life, wisdom and other goods it 'belongs' to individuals – but also collectively to all of us. Neither government nor collections of privileged individuals have the right to impose damaging competitive systems. Or so I would argue. As I stated in the previous chapter, education is an intrinsic personal benefit to all the many diverse individuals who are engaged in teaching and learning; but also it is essential to society as a whole, economically and politically. Therefore, it belongs both to individuals and to the community. A just society has to resolve the possible tension between benefits for individuals and their society to the satisfaction of both. In this chapter, I begin to explore this tension and its possible resolution, by putting forward a view of individuals and their relationship to the society they inhabit. I use arguments by political philosophers, and also include stories by teachers and learners who have struggled to get an education of their own, and to help others to do the same.

Edwin Maxwell. We were all walking in one direction

The music teacher spent much of his music lessons by having us as students coming into his class and sitting there with our arms folded. For all the lesson you had to sit there in silence while he got on with something else. Now if any of you made any noises or anything you were held in detention as punishment. One boy – a very funny guy, well he seemed funny at that time – used to make faces and you used to giggle out of context. Then: Wham! A detention! It might still seem funny in a way, but I was first exposed to the waste when I was about 14.

My sister went to a different school and she came home with her homework. Homework was like a new discovery to me. She was being taught music and how to read music and having to recognize things I only saw on sheets – not understanding what it was about, and why they had five lines and crochets and quavers. I was never taught that. My sister's homework taught me things like that. I was cheated. We had this teacher who took us for three years and never taught us anything like that. He was wasting my time.

There was a group of us boys, we used to walk through Mapperley Park to the school I went to. We were all walking in one direction. Many of the kids from Mapperley Park went to the Boys' High School or the Girls' High School (where my daughter ended up, I might add). We were going one way – totally opposite to them. We saw them as the posh kids and we were quite different: not knowing what the end product was like but they would just seem completely elevated and different to us. We were passing in the opposite direction. There were no discussions, nothing. The only thing: we used to occasionally bump into them and nick their Parker pens and stuff like that and think, 'Wow! Great!' We'd not seen the parallels or consequences. It was the complete reverse, the experiences.

Then a few years ago Jennifer [see Chapter 1] was being inspired to go on further at university, and here she was wanting to take note of my opinion. She was coming home and she was talking things through with me. Here was I offering encouragement. She was doing something that I felt I was completely barred from doing because I wasn't set up in life to go to university. University was something for other people. It was never something I could do.

Self-confidence is one of the things I have always had. I was dead cocky about certain things. I had started in business. I had gone from the point of starting a company as an electrician, working alongside people, renovating my own premises. There were a load of housing grants flowing around for refurbishment at that point. So I reassessed what I was doing: I was really a building contractor. I did that and it delivered every time. I thought, 'My God, my future is wrapped up!' Then suddenly came the recession. The future was only upwards and then we hit this recession. Gradually things became a liability. I thought that everything that I had done up until then had been intuitive, and that perhaps it might have been different had I had a little bit of insight and training as to the theoretical side. I might have navigated differently. I might have come out less scarred than I did. I didn't have the necessary qualifications to get on the MBA programme. What I had then was just the craft-based training I had before my apprenticeship. I had the experience, which was the high point – so I got on to the diploma with APEL.

The first year of the diploma helped me greatly. It meant I was able to put things into context. I was able to start to look at my situation and start to analyse it in greater depth. The second year was even better. What I learnt was the processes and functions of management from a theoretical base and I had never thought about that. Suddenly all the things I did intuitively I was able to relate to theory. I'd found an interest. I really did. That fuelled me more and more to find out. Everything I was led to do I could relate back to my own business cases and I really enjoyed that.

Smooth talk and irregular tales

The discourse of education policy is, unfortunately, smoothed and spun. The abstract individual of classic liberal theory, who is distinguishable only by his preferences, seems to have a new lease of life in the idealized child and the idealized student of educational policy-making. It is a kind of smoothing out that is needed to fit everyone into a format of standards, a uniform trajectory within uniform systems, marked by zero tolerance and best practice. The talk in Britain is of examinations (baseline assessments, SATs, GCSEs – O, A/S, A – NVQs)[1] and of competencies, benchmarks and performance indicators.

Details that disrupt the smoothness get left out. So, not surprisingly, such discourse has little to contribute about how to live with diversity. The discourse cannot survive an encounter with real people. As Ball *et al.* (2000: 16) remark, even relatively complex theory struggles:

> Our various attempts at analysis and interpretation have been continually confronted by the obdurate diversity of our data. That diversity refers both to the variety of trajectories and positions occupied by the young people in the study as well as to the range of data, over time and across topics, amassed for each of the young people.

I have referred to the British context but smooth talk is not confined to those islands. For instance, this is what Maxine Greene (1995: 17–18) says about Goals 2000: The Educate America Act:

> This act has now been legislated into federal law. It sets forth national goals for education, intended to be achieved in five years . . . This is presented as the new national agenda for education and the presumption is that it is realizable, poverty and inequality notwithstanding.

One problem has to do with the implication that standards and tests can simply be imposed; another has to do with the so far untapped diversity among American youth today – its still undefined talents and energies, its differentiated modes of expression . . . [So] I begin to seek out ways in which the arts, in particular, can release imagination to open new perspectives, to identify alternatives . . . [that] keep human beings and their cultures alive.

It is vital to recognize the complexity of human beings: partly in order to recognize the world as it is; partly because the idealized smooth discourse that drowns out other voices is one that reflects the lived realities of the more powerful, richer and privileged members of a society. Other less powerful, less privileged people find it hard to talk to each other over their loud voices. That is, they – we – need to hear their voices among the many, instead of not being able to hear them at all. Here is Ahdaf Soueif, an Egyptian novelist now living in London, on why the al-Jazeera TV station is so important to her and to other Arabs (Soueif 2001).

For us outside [the Arab world; that is, those living in the West], it provides the one window through which we can breathe. It also provides reassurance against the negative or partial image of ourselves constantly beamed at us every day from the media of whatever country we happen to find ourselves in. It's not that we want to hear our own opinions; rather we want to hear a variety of opinions of which ours is one. The titles of some of their most popular programmes speak for themselves: Against the Current, The Opposite Direction, One Opinion and Another, and so on.

The tales woven into Part 1 of this book could easily share these titles. They, too, are often against the current, even in the opposite direction, and are certainly one opinion and another. They are certainly not part of the idealized language of education, which smoothes out difference or confines it to a few large categories.

Anne Seller. Space to dream

I was born in a small Yorkshire town. My father was a lance corporal and my mother was a nurse. After the war he became a teacher and she became a factory worker. I grew up in a village near Bedford.

Black, working-class, 'other' women: they all have an identity they can be proud of. There's an asymmetry here – and a problem, which shows itself clearly in discussions: 'I'm proud of being working class, and I don't want that made invisible.' But also: 'I came to college because I was fed up.' Class, in this country at any rate, means we despise our own roots and feel guilty about it. We love our people and seek to escape their lives. Our first experiences of repression are through our families and neighbours. And for many, school is an escape, and is represented as a way out. You dream of a different life, and a good socialist would say that can only be achieved collectively. Stay in your street and work for it. Where I came from, you had to leave to get the space to dream. And the universities gave you that. At the same time, there was a high cost of entry: a lot of self-denial. And when somebody else, however subtly, requires of you that you change, especially your personal habits (your speech, your clothes, your meal-times), you begin to say: 'But who I am is . . . and I don't intend to forget it.'

That isn't true of me. I went for space, and I paid a high cost. But, in those years, I did not look back at all, and I felt I came from a background with no culture. My family didn't have sing-songs in pubs, but the Home Service, 'O, My Papa' and The Archers, worries over money and respectability, and the importance of 'getting on'. I wanted conversation and ideas and poetry and angry paintings and a wider world, and could only see how to get it through the approved channels: a degree and/or marriage. I looked at men in terms of who their friends were.

We have 'coming home' experiences: moments of discovering who we are, and where we belong. And I find those places with relief, satisfaction, with a sense of 'this is what I have been searching for, without knowing it'. They have not been places of rest, safety, comfort. Coming home has been coming to the place where my work in the world is, and such work can be risky and dangerous and hard. But this is also the place where my self is safe, where I am no longer lost, no longer carried along as the jetsam on the floods of this moment, this society.

Some examples of moments when I found, and lost, my homes. At university, the freshers' fair. I had worked and looked for a way of being in the political world, of reaching beyond family. I had gone to the only place there was in a small rural community, the Young Conservatives, seeking there not the politics of power, but of principle. (I couldn't have used those words then.) I came across the CND stall and a person said, 'But you can't believe it right to use this bomb.' I didn't believe it, but now I found, for the first time, others whose lives were organized round that belief. I no longer had to try to convert the Tory Party on my own, indeed I could leave it.

I discovered a self there, an identity, and I based my politics on that self. I went with people who were like me and almost killed that self in the process. Other stories: at about the same time I found philosophy, another coming home; people taking seriously the questions I had been asking, further alienation from my family, from that larger society, further risk of self, and almost loss of self. For it meant subscription to a narrow rationality which rendered the questions of my life mean-ingless. But it was also my home and I kept trying to revive those questions in an acceptable language. People never understood my excitement at the very big questions, where it seemed metaphysics might be revived. Then there were the people I identified with: well you had to go to the root causes of war, of armaments, but that meant engagement in a politics of contempt which was far from the home I had felt on the march from Aldermaston. So coming home is highly risky; you can be mistaken about the home that you have come to, and lose your self as quickly as you find her. I nearly disappeared in cynicism and despair. Feminism and the wilderness saved me.

At the deepest level, this coming home enables me to see that I am not in the world on pain of good behaviour: I don't have to prove myself to anyone, or to meet their expectations to be allowed in. I don't have to believe that the price of access is to disguise most of what I am, to measure up to the gatekeeper's code. Liberation comes in feeling that code to be irrelevant. I distinguish that from emancipation, which is the ending of the code altogether, and includes liberation.

Story makers: an education of one's own

Any set of human beings will be individually different from each other. Some of these differences derive from the socio-political context. Some are personal. Both kinds of difference influence how people can set about making their own education what they want it to be. Ahdaf Soueif writes as an Egyptian, as an Arab, as a woman, as an expatriate. She cannot be contained in any of these descriptions. Equally, she is in all of them in the sense that they are not just superficial features of her self. It is hard for any of us to imagine who we might be if we could change our nationality, our race, our sex, or if we moved to some other part of the world to live.

The philosopher Hannah Arendt was never going to be able to escape the issue of diversity. It assailed her as a Jew in Germany in the first half of the twentieth century, as a woman in philosophy, as a foreigner – a German intellectual – in the USA. She never quite fitted the norm for any of these, but never wanted to deny any of them as parts of who she was. It is not surprising then that she developed illuminating ways to explain how a person deals with being an exception to the norm.

She uses the useful concepts of the 'parvenu', 'the pariah' and the 'exception Jew' in order to explain the framework of options open to minorities within a majority culture, whether or not they have been settled for generations, when they do not have the option of being invisible. The analysis begins with a history of Jews in Germany from the beginning of the nineteenth century. Jews were accepted in non-Jewish society, only if: (a) they were not like the mass of other Jews (exceptions); and (b) they retained their foreign, 'exotic' appeal (Arendt 1973: 56–7). Thus, 'exception Jews' were required to (feel themselves to) be exceptions from the Jewish people and also exceptional human beings, financially or intellectually. Thus, anyone who chose to become a 'parvenu' had both to deny and to assert their Jewishness in ways that suited the majority. The alternative was to remain a pariah – outside majority culture altogether. This option, at least, allowed for political action, but only if the pariah became (to use Lazare's term) a 'conscious pariah' (Arendt 1973: 65).

Arendt also argues for understanding the importance both of 'who you are' and of 'what you are'. She argues that both are necessary parts of action and speech and of the relationships which depend on them. That is, all people are unique and they reveal their unique personal identities – *who they are* – in what they say and do. At the same time, to be human is to be in relationship, in a culture – and this influences *what they are*. The 'who' and the 'what' both need to be acknowledged in any relationship. She refers to Jews and Negroes as examples, pointing out that while being seen only as a racial 'what' is dehumanizing, political speech and action depend on affirming the cultural base of being human. (See quotes in Chapter 5.)

The stories in Part 1 of this book reveal different people – different in 'who' they are, and also different in 'what' they are – as they act in relation to learning and to education systems. The stories are told in relation to particular historical, political, social and national contexts. Social class, race, gender and education policies: they all combine to affect the outcome of the stories. The stories tell of getting an education of one's own, and of how far each person was able to do that, within the bounds that constrained them.

Perry Taylor. Happy learning what I want to learn

I did well in school. I studied everything that I had got to. I struggled with a lot of things, especially maths. It always took a long time for anything to do with maths to sink in. Each new topic that was brought up, I would sit there looking blank and think to myself, 'Down the library tonight, get a maths book out and read that chapter on what they have been saying to me.' That's what I used to do. I used to study an *Idiot's Guide to Maths* sort of book to figure out what they had been saying in class. I would get over that hurdle and then the next time we would have a maths lesson it was something completely different and I would think to myself, 'Oh my God! Back down the library again!' I used to spend hours poring through books until I understood what the teacher was flipping saying in class and that's how I did it.

I was never interested in languages at all. The only language that we were offered was French. I had no interest in it at all, mainly because I thought to myself, 'Well, what is the point? I am never going to go abroad.' Because there were only a couple of middle-class people who were going abroad then. Such as us, working-class people, we never went abroad. We went down to the east coast for the weekend or for a week. So I thought to myself, 'Well, why wrap myself up with this when I am never going to use it? I am probably never even going to meet a French person. What I need to study is maths and science and get that sorted out, get my priorities right.' So that's what I did. I came away from school with quite good results but it was due to getting books out and studying things for myself, catching up on things that I didn't understand in class, from when I got home till 10 o'clock at night, just to get things sorted out. When I left school, all the doubts about what I had been learning came true because I ended up down the pit.

When I left school I thought to myself, 'Thank God I have done with that!' I was sick of poring through books, studying things that I never thought I would use.

The things that I have learned since are things that I have learned because I find them interesting, such as languages. I started with Spanish. The second holiday that we had abroad, the apartment was broken into during the night. Therefore, the next morning we had to go looking for a police station. We didn't speak a word of Spanish apart from 'yes' and 'thank you'; so trying to ask people the way to the police station was such a hard job. We were finally helped by somebody. A lady was crossing the road. She must have seen that we were looking lost and she asked in probably five or six languages what we were. I thought to myself, My God! Five or six languages – all those languages that she knows! She gave us directions to the police station in English. I don't know what nationality she was. Basically, that's where it all started. There are a lot of sites on the Internet that have got sound files that will give you native speakers telling you how words are pronounced and how letters are pronounced. Then I started looking at Dutch as well because the Dutch people that I have met have all been so nice – and why should everybody speak English?

I started looking at things and learning things when I was the security officer down at Clifton Hall. You had got plenty of time on your own. If it was quiet, and you hadn't got any hassle from the kids on the estate, you had got a good few hours doing nothing. I couldn't just sit and look at the clock going round. So I started thinking about what I could do to put that spare time to use. The first thing that I did was to learn how to use the computer – people had shown me little bits here and there – once everybody had gone, just playing around with it on my own to see what I could make it do. Enough to get by: I am not a computer wizard. I was spending hours playing around with the computer to see what it did. Then I found the net and found music sites on it, basically looking for information on rock and roll singers. Then one link led to another and I found music.

I never liked music at school. I hated it. But then again, what 15-year-old kids like listening to Chopin? Sat bolt upright, silent and listening to classical music playing. Then you had to write an essay about it afterwards. I didn't know what to write at that age. It was boring. It was just something else that got in the way of the things like maths, science and English. I wasn't interested at all.

But then I found these sites, and I thought, 'I'll get myself a guitar.' I got myself a guitar and I learned to read a bit of music. I learned the chords from the net – printed chord charts off the net. I sat there learning chords till my fingers were red raw. Then I started thinking to myself, I shouldn't mind playing the double bass.

They have got stage presence. Very few people remember double bass players – but they always remember somebody playing double bass on the stage and think-ing, 'Oo, that was good!' So I got myself a double bass and spent hours at night learning how to play that. I did get quite good at reading double bass music. Then I ended up playing in a band.

Then after the double bass I got on to the languages. I don't know what's going to be next. If it is interesting, it's worth doing. If it is not then it's just hard work. And none of us really like hard work. It's like the staff development courses. The line managers always try to send you on courses: 'Get yourself a paper for this. Get yourself a paper for that.' I'm not interested. I'm going nowhere. I am quite happy here. I am quite happy learning what I want to learn and not what they want me to learn, so that they can hold a flag up and say, 'Look, our people are doing this.'

Situated stories: an education for each and everyone

Arendt focuses on Jews, especially in Europe, and also on race relations in the United States of America. Her work preceded current equality/difference debates: she was writing in the 1950s and 1960s, in the shadow of her experi-ences of Nazi totalitarianism. She says very little indeed about other differ-ences. For instance, she was not a feminist, and had little to say about gender relations.

Since the 1950s, the theorization of equality/difference has progressed in leaps and bounds. We can now see that it is only rarely that one difference dominates, as it did for the Jews in Nazi Germany. In the 1970s and 1980s, there was an explosion of interest in a wide range of differences: race, religion, class, gender, sexuality and disability were the most prominent. It became difficult to deal with this range, politically. In schools, for instance, equal opportunities policies became enmeshed in such questions. Bitter arguments broke out about which difference was prior and about which form of dis-crimination was the most pernicious. In the 1980s and 1990s, 'hyphenated identities' began to proliferate, as it became obvious how many axes of differ-ence there were, and so how many different combinations were possible. The sheer number of combinations led to rethinking how to deal with difference. Thankfully, the continuing ferment is leading to a much better understanding of the issues and how to deal with them.

Realization has grown that group membership is plural, complex and con-tinually under construction. Groups are formed in different ways. We are socially positioned in some of them, whether we like it or not, on the basis of attributes such as skin colour, accent, sexual preference, disability and nationality. Some such groups are treated with (dis)respect and/or are materi-ally (dis)advantaged. Some members affirm, while others resist their group ascriptions, or even remain unconscious of their membership. There are other groups that form from a commonality of experience, language, history and so on. Again, some of these are treated with (dis)respect and/or are materially (dis)advantaged. Again, members may affirm, resist or ignore their memberships. To help work with this complexity, Fraser (1997) has helpfully suggested using the analytical dimensions 'cultural' and 'structural'. All groups include both, but some, like groups based on sexuality, tend to be more cultural, and some, like those based on social class, to be more structural. Race and gender score high on both dimensions.

Young (2000: 88–9) explains the damaging, misleading effects of attempting to fix group identities:

> Everyone relates to a plurality of social groups; every social group has other social groups cutting across it . . . The attempt to define a common group identity tends to normalize the experience and perspective of some group members while marginalizing or silencing others.

Since each member of any group will also belong to other groups, no one solution will fit all. Unfortunately, education policy – when it is forced to notice diversity – smoothes out plurality by focusing on only one axis of difference. A favourite is 'boys' and their 'under-achievement'. As if social class, ethnicity and sexuality had no influence on school performance. As if what is significant for some boys would be significant for all. As if all boys related to masculinity in the same way. As if there were only one kind of masculinity.

For equality to work, it is important to see that the problems of justice that groups face will not necessarily be amenable to similar solutions in terms of voice, recognition and material redistribution. Nor will one view represent all members of a group. The first requirement is for an equal say, in order that different points of view can be expressed.

Rita Dobbins. I can do it regardless of anyone or anything

I was very bright as a child. I had read *Pilgrim's Progress* by the time I was seven. I used to read and read and read and read. I couldn't wait to get to school. I started school at Easter as soon as I was four – my birthday is in March – and I loved it. I was in my element until I passed the 11 plus and went to the grammar school and I hated it. The girls in the class were snobs. My mum was by herself with me and my brother and I had free school dinners. Not only were a lot of the girls in my class very snobbish but likewise the teachers.

My form mistress was an absolute cow. I tell you this. If I saw her on the street now I would try and run her over. She made my life a misery. I used to have to queue up on a Monday morning while everybody else had paid their dinner money. I then was sent to queue up in the main entrance hall outside the office to get my dinner tickets. I was the only girl in school that had free school dinners. For years she wasn't my form teacher, she was a cookery teacher. When we did the cookery lessons and you had to bring your stuff in, the school fund paid for my cookery ingredients. I had to go out to a little local shop and buy them but not until after we had done the theory bit and the practical demonstration. Then she said, 'You can start cooking. Rita, here's the money to go to the shop for your ingredients.' My cookery was always the very last because other girls had done half their preparation by the time I got started.

In needlework she was the same teacher again. She had to go to town with me one term to buy some material and a pattern. So we got into this little shop in town and I decided that I liked this red wool material – bright scarlet wool.

'No you can't have that. You can have this one.'

'I don't like that.'

'You can have this one.'

A really dull grey-brown. I wanted this scarlet. It was gorgeous. So she finally gave in, bought me the material and pattern for an eight-gore skirt with big patch pockets on. By this time (I was 14) I was already making my own clothes. The first week we laid it out flat and pinned the pattern on, the second week we cut it out and the third week we did all the tailor's tacks. After the third week, when I'd sat looking out of the window for hours because I was bored, I took it home and finished it. I used my friend's sewing machine and put three layers of beautiful machine embroidery around the edge of the patch pockets. I wore it for an hour as well and showed it off. I was so proud of it.

When I went back to school the next week she made me unpick it. The only bit she didn't make me unpick was the machine embroidery. I had to unpick everything else, take the zip out, everything, because I had done it without her saying I could. I had not done it in class. So I laid this material out in its pieces on the table every week for the rest of the term and I never touched it. I just sat and looked out the window. I never sewed it up again. I threw it in the bin. And it was beautiful material. It really was.

I also opted out of the maths. It was a different teacher. She would give me this work to do. It would take me about two minutes and there the answers were in my head. But I didn't sit and do all the working out on the papers and so she marked them all wrong. The right answer was there but I hadn't shown her how I had got that answer, so she wouldn't mark them right. So after about a month of this, I stopped doing any homework and I never did any homework. When it came to that year's maths exam I actually got 15 per cent. She was marking the papers. I read the question and I wrote the answers, but she wanted it all worked out properly. When we had to decide what we were doing for O-levels would you believe they let me give up maths? So I never did any more after that year. So I've still never got a maths O-level. I didn't take my O-levels at school. I opted out at 15. Now do you think if I had had a good teacher I might have been a bloody genius?

I had a lovely English teacher. The first year English teacher was wonderful. She gave us all a book. 'This is the book we are doing in class, and this is a book for you to read.' The next class we had was two days away and I took both books back in. 'I've read these.' She took me in the store cupboard – and I had a new book every day for two terms until I had read every book in the store cupboard. I thought she was wonderful.

I am obstinate and I will not back down. I have got half an Open University psychology degree. I broke my leg a month before summer school. Now, summer school was at Brighton. It is a big campus and I thought I can't cope. So I told my tutor I wasn't going to summer school but he never quite passed the message on to the right people at the right time. So they still sent me the summer school bill and I refused to pay it. And they chuntered and chuntered and I said, 'No, I am not paying it because I didn't go and my tutor knew I wasn't going.'

'If you don't pay it you are not getting next year's course.'

'Well, sod you then, I'll leave it, I'm not bothering.'

I stopped dead and I've never done any more with it. All that work: hours and hours and hours.

At this stage although I have never actually done anything officially, I have had quite a good education. And the satisfaction of knowing that if I want to do something I *can* do it. Regardless of anybody or anything.

An equal say: an education of our own

For any group of people to get an education of their own, the first need is to have a say and to have it listened to. It is easy for people to benefit from their formal education if they are offered respect and adequate resources. These are there for some social/political groups. They are missing for others, as is clear from some of the stories told in this book. The issue is usually expressed in terms of the needs for social/political groups to get both respectful treatment and also a fair share of available resources: both recognition and redistribution. The wide understanding that both recognition and redistribution are needed has come about because those without them have said so. In other words, they felt the need and expressed it. Some groups, of course, have been able to express their need more forcibly. They have had their say. Any group wanting to influence the education available to them – to get an education of their own – needs a say.

It might be thought that having a say is a matter of being empowered by someone else: of being given skills and space by someone more powerful. This is misleading. To have a say is, precisely, to challenge the more powerful – who got power by dominating available air spaces. More powerful people have, of course, choices about how to exercise it, including in ways that will give up some of their airtime. Having a say is learnt in relationship, with and against others. As Arendt (1958: 190) writes:

> Action . . . always establishes relationships and therefore has an inherent tendency to force open all limitations and cut across all boundaries . . . [that] exist within the realm of human affairs, but they never offer a framework that can reliably withstand the onslaught with which each new generation must insert itself.

But what does it mean to have a say? There are many ways in which lack of respect and lack of resources combine to prevent people from expressing themselves. First, perniciously, some people do not think they have anything worth saying: that they are too unimportant. Second, some people are silenced by expectations governing who gets to express themselves in particular contexts. No wonder that the idea of 'coming to voice' has been so powerful in the past few decades. Lastly, it is possible to speak, eloquently and persuasively – but still the audience pays no serious attention. As Spivak (1990: 59) wrote:

> For me, the question 'Who should speak?' is less crucial that 'Who will listen?' . . . the real demand is that, when I speak from that position [as a Third World person] I should be listened to seriously.

Certain conditions are needed – or must be demanded – if the audience is to hear. First, there is a requirement for what Young (2000: 58) calls 'greeting'. As she points out, without acknowledgement of the other as a subject rather than an object, communication is distorted. It is equally distorted if the person is not then taken seriously. When Jennifer Maxwell (Chapter 1) says her parents were too respectful, surely more significant is that the officials were not respectful enough. Nada Trikić (Chapter 3) points out the disrespect accorded her father once his foreign accent is heard. A spokesperson for a whole group needs acknowledgement of that group – but also has to accord the same respect to the group members. (For some of the complexities of representation see Phillips 1995.)

Second, if the audience is to hear, it has a responsibility to take seriously whatever forms of expression are used. Academics typically like to use academic prose to make their arguments. But there are other forms. All the riches of human expression are available, from narrative and drama, through song and dance, to cartoons and gestures. Sometimes a person or group has to use whatever form of expression is available: Jennifer Maxwell (Chapter 1) bit her teacher; Sharon Baillon (Chapter 4) opted out. Both were expressing their views of the education on offer. It seems that Jennifer, but not Sharon, was listened to seriously.

Syble Morgan. Looking out for the best for the children

I've always been very active in the community. It has helped me that somewhere you can find people to work with on areas that bother you for the community: not just for yourself but for the community, even if you yourself can step away from these situations. It's how much you can do for, or how much you can help other people to help themselves. That's what it's about, actually.

The Marcus Garvey Nursery was set up in the seventies after a long-drawn-out time begging and fund raising. We managed to get a building of our own. We opened in October 1976. This was the fruit of 1973, when Black children were under-achieving, when paraffin heater fires were claiming lives and maiming Black children and when we were told as a people in the community that we only wanted things – that we weren't doing anything for ourselves. I must say that Black people could only get cleaning jobs. It was generally thought that if you were Black then you were bad. And I remember a councillor telling me that racism was not as bad as I explained it: it was just my imagination and I was paranoid. That is the background in which the Marcus Garvey Nursery was set up.

We fought tooth and nail to have a black nursery with Black staff. Now, the climate didn't allow us to set up a nursery for anybody else but Blacks because white people wouldn't bring their children there. Not in those days. Not when we started. I stayed there for eight years and in about the sixth year I had both Asians and white children. Maybe that was when society wasn't so afraid of us any more.

At the same time, there were studies in America. The children from the Caribbean, especially Jamaica, did as well in America as they did at home – and better because they had better opportunities. Yet our children here were leaving school and some of them did not even know how to sign their names. Now I'm not putting all that on the authorities, because I always wonder: 'How come this parent didn't know that the child can't read before he left school?' But then again, it is the way we see things. We are accustomed to give up our children to the teachers alone. And the teachers are going to be there looking out for the best for the children. That's what happened when we came here. But the teachers didn't even understand them, never mind looking out for their well-being. Therefore our ethos for the nursery was to care for the child seven, eight hours a day. And the playing had to be mixed with education from the word go. We didn't take them and teach them – put them to sit down and teach them – but we designed our own way of them learning their alphabet and knowing how to count, of being acquainted with what's going on around them and in the world.

There was a very vibrant parent group. Our parents did not want to come on the management committee [of Harambee, the parent organization that started the nursery]. Most of them, God bless them, they were so glad that Black people were setting up something for Black people – that Black people were setting up something; that they could get into a group and help themselves – that they'd present themselves to do what they could do and what they feel happy doing. So they would help with the cleaning. I could send them shopping. I could ask them to come in, under supervision, if I had a member of staff out.

And I could help them with dealing with the system, with the children, their other children that were in school or whatever was happening. I could encourage them to go to parents' evenings and to ask questions, whether they get a proper answer or no, but still ask questions. Because then, too, was the time when, when teachers were saying that Black people don't come to parents' evenings. Now, a lot of Black people in those times worked at night. So it was hard for them to come, to get to open evenings. Funnily enough when it reached the stages when Black parents were going into school and the teacher was saying, 'Oh Johnny is doing very good work,' and we were asking, 'Which standard of good: the white standard or the Black standard?', it wasn't taken up.

I know a lot of the parents who brought their children to Marcus Garvey. There is evidence of a lot of educational achievement. But then when I started working in, well, nurseries of the system, I realized the difference. There are children that came to Marcus Garvey that would do well anywhere, because their parents were professionals, but then those were the children who left the nursery reading. The others that didn't leave there reading, or that didn't have professional parents, they have made the grade just as well. And in our community, I must say, it's not just the ones that make it to university with all the odds against them; it's the ones that keep themselves out of the madhouse and out of the prison, that I think are still successful, because this society is geared against us.

Using differences in a transversal politics: an education for all

An education suitable for *all* learners – good for each and good for everyone – requires everyone to take account of the real differences between them, however they are expressed. This is not ever going to be a cosy, consensual process, even in theory. It is plainly more difficult, practically, than getting agreement among a homogeneous group. It is plainly more difficult, theoretically, than assuming that 'rational men will agree'. Difference includes differences in what counts as a good rational argument. Therefore, plurality means acknowledging others, and listening seriously to them, even where there are difficult, heartfelt disagreements to resolve. This is so difficult because, as Fraser puts it, what is then implied is actions in the political, not mere tolerance. Politics as usual depends on voting, on co-option, on coalition. These work by containing difference as much as by taking it seriously.

New forms of politics are required. One such is 'transversal politics', which has been developed through theorizing from real experiences and struggles to take joint action across difference. Cynthia Cockburn and Lynnette Hunter

(1999: 89) define it as 'the practice of creatively crossing (and re-drawing) the borders that mark significant politicised differences'. They have drawn on a project that both learned from and helped women carrying out joint projects across racialized ethnic/religious divides in Northern Ireland, Bosnia and Israel. Other projects have been carried out in various areas where difference is serious enough to be a killing matter. Forms of expression included not only talking but also creative writing, theatre and photographic exhibitions. The essence of these projects was that they worked across differences that could not be ignored. Mere friendliness was not enough: as one of the Israeli women put it, 'the issue is not social but political' (Cockburn 1998: 211).

Central to doing transversal politics is keeping differences deconstructed, rather than solidifying or reifying them. Cockburn gives examples of how the women in the project consistently refused simple descriptors of identity, and, she argues, this was crucial to their being able to continue working together constructively (Cockburn 1998: 225):

> A woman will wait to hear the other's telling of history, her view of the event, idea of herself, reading of the situation, preference for action – rather than making suppositions because she 'is' Catholic/Croat/Jew.

Similarly, Fraser argues that the best chance of dealing with both the cultural and the structural dimensions of difference is to work towards transformation in both, in ways that blur group differentiations through socialism and deconstruction. In other words, politics depends on: opening up, not closing down; engaging with a response, rather than predetermining it; working with a 'rough and ready provisional agreement' (Young 2000); admitting complexity rather than keeping it at bay by smoothing it over.

Educators learn to work across differences. Their work may not be carried out in life-threatening circumstances, but it certainly has profound consequences for lives. Surely a form of transversal politics, actions in the political, is crucial in getting an education for all. This is not just a matter for policy makers or for pressure groups: the Ministry or the parents' association. It is also for all levels of the educational system: classrooms and schools; universities and community organizations; local and central government.

Maxine Greene. Breaking through the crust

I remember my earliest paper, I think, or one of the earliest, when I was trying to get into philosophy of education under the cold hand of analytic philosophy (with those analysts – all male, all big drinkers and smokers, all nice guys – holding private meetings in hotel rooms, talking Ayers and Ryle, as if they were in a locker room telling dirty jokes). Anyway, the paper I had in mind was 'The meaning of meaninglessness'. It showed people I was 'soft', too 'literary' and, by implication, too 'female'. And I was scared to death, thinking back nostalgically to the days when I liked being introduced as a woman who 'thinks like a man' – and felt like curtseying in gratitude for the compliment. It once happened in Hawaii, and I can still smell the heavy scent of the lei around my neck – and feel the guilt washing over me.

At Barnard, I had majored in history, minored in philosophy, never thought for a single minute of education, but what the hell. Next year I was assistant in that class, suddenly teaching big classes mostly in history of education, realized I could get my doctorate without charging my husband. I guess it was there that I first read Sartre, began my philosophical marginalization. I did a long thesis trying to please my fatherly sponsor (oh spare me) on 'Naturalist humanism in eighteenth-century England, 1750–1780: an essay in the sociology of knowledge', only because he wanted me to do a thesis on Henry Fielding, whom he had just discovered, and I did want to please him but go beyond, way, way beyond into all kinds of inter-disciplinary stuff, art, philosophy, politics, even rotten boroughs, believe it or not, and Coleridge on romanticism. Anyway, a woman in philosophy of education in 1955 did not have a chance of a job. So I took one (a long, long drive from home) teaching world literature in New Jersey. I had never taken a course in English, had a marvellous year doing self-study in world lit. from Homer on, learned much, left partly because the club where Faculty ate would not admit Jews, nor would the golf club etc. I went back to NYU part-time, got kicked out of philosophy because of being too literary, soft *et al.* (again), finally got to Brooklyn College teaching foundations, then to Teacher College to be editor of the *TC Record*. I had been president of the Philosophy of Education Society by then but Teacher College's Department of Philosophy and the Social Sciences had never hired a woman, so I took a job in English (seduced by false promises) with permission to teach one course in philosophy. I won't go on. It took 10 years, I guess, before I was allowed into that department, was given a chair, had huge courses. When in the English Department, because I wanted to keep one foot in philosophy, I asked to teach a course in philosophy and literature. The Chair asked, 'Philosophy-and or philosophy-of?' 'Of,' I said (luckily). And there I was teaching myself aesthetics and education, helping invent the Lincoln Center Institute,[2] writing, speaking in the field.

I am interested in the ways to create the spaces through the arts to see differ-ently, to break through the crust. The alternative to fixities, to reification, is seeing differently, by all means available. To continue to struggle for all this, for the arts, for social justice is to continue to struggle to protect the spaces where people can come to be. Relevant here is my long connection with the Lincoln Center Institute for the Arts in Education and the Center for Social Imagination, in which I relate my concern with the arts, aesthetics *et al.* to a concern for social justice and social action. I suppose these are both concerns with what Freire calls the process of 'conscientization', which I call 'wide-awakeness' a lot of the time. I have been the 'philosopher-in-residence' at the Lincoln Center Institute for the Arts in Education, mostly a three-week summer programme in which teachers work with professional artists in workshops, see exhibitions, see/hear performances, hear me on a kind of rudimentary aesthetics – and, in winter, artists come to schools to invent relevant multicultural, multi-age programmes.

Education and social justice

In this chapter I have discussed opening up education. The discussion moved from a reminder of the diversity of learners and their teachers, to a consideration of how each one of them could get 'an education of my own'. Then this idea was developed from 'my own' into 'our own' and finally how 'our own' could meet with other perspectives on education to develop an education for all. This development made use of ideas about how individuals and groups might connect with each other, in ways that acknowledge power and difference, for their common good. Therefore, I have necessarily started to talk about 'social justice'. In the next chapter I look more closely at how it has been theorized, and what kind of theory would be useful in the struggle against injustices in education.

Notes

1 Standard Attainment Targets; General Certificate of Secondary Education at Ordinary Level, Advanced Subsidiary Level and Advanced Level.
2 Working in the tradition of Dewey, James and the existentialists, the Center brings schoolchildren, artists, academics and social activists together in conferences and workshops to explore possibilities of reform and transformation in schools and social communities.

3 Really useful theories of social justice

Loose talk about social justice in education

Educational theorists in the 1950s and 1960s used to discuss 'social justice', referring only to questions of social class. In the 1970s and 1980s came the inclusion of gender and race (unfortunately often elbowing out attention to social class) as areas of discrimination, exclusions and non-recognition. This change was marked by the term 'equality', which became the usual term used as an organizing concept. During the 1980s and 1990s there was an increasing realization that different claims for equality (class, race, gender, sexuality and disability) could not easily be dealt with together. The different claims were not all aimed at the same set of issues, but neither were they all totally different – some claims overlapped. Racial discrimination, for instance, is not quite the same as discrimination on the grounds of sexuality or learning difficulties. Indeed, all racial discrimination is not the same. Rather than simply talking of 'racism', there is a move to talk of 'racisms'. (For example, distinctions are drawn between 'colour racism' and 'cultural racism'.) In the 1990s 'social justice' re-emerged as an organizing concept. The use of the term 'social justice' allows for a rethinking of the place that social class, race and the rest occupy in relation to injustices in education. However, unhappily, it may have gained some of its currency because it can be used to speak in very general terms, sliding over difficult political, practical issues. No wonder that some activists prefer to stick to specificities like 'racial equality' or 'gay pride'.

The lack of an agreed terminology means that injustice is described in terms which are highly political, fluid and slippery. Here is a stated view of a politician in Britain:

> At the heart of all our work is one central theme: national renewal. Britain built as one nation, in which every citizen is valued and has a stake; in which no one is excluded from opportunity . . . in which we

> make it ... our national purpose to tackle social division and inequality.

This excerpt is taken from a speech by Tony Blair, when as the British Prime Minister he launched the Social Exclusion Unit in 1997. The quotation was used as an epigraph by David Blunkett, when Secretary of State for Education, in a speech on empowering people and communities. He picked up the same themes and enlarged on them, mentioning 'nationhood', 'division and inequality', 'children born into poverty', 'everyone into work as a means of empowerment'. He said (Blunkett 1999):

> This is not just an issue of social justice. The economic costs of this waste of human potential are huge ... As a country, we need the effort and skill of all our people to compete and succeed ... Life-long learning ... is vital across the age groups.

This speech illustrates some of the problem. The political rhetoric, the blurring and ambiguity of terms – such as 'citizen', 'social division', 'social justice', 'economics' and 'all our people' – all combine to make it difficult to join in the discussion. I want to ask, for instance, 'Where do asylum seekers fit in?', 'What kind of social division is meant if there is a difference between division and inequality?', 'Isn't the economic life of the nation part of social justice?' and 'Need life-long learning be primarily directed towards economic activity?' These questions can be asked – I have just done so – but it is a continuing effort to do so, to use words in a more precise and careful way.

There is a general need for more precise, more careful, more coherent ways of talking. There is a specific need in educational contexts for a useful theory that will get action in schools, in colleges, in universities and in community groups: a theory that is accountable to all the people it encompasses. There are plenty of theories of social justice available, but only some of them will be useful for those particular purposes.

Nada Trikić. What's all this about?

I think my own personal experience of education has ensured that I've got an edge in terms of fair play and opportunities: being somebody who failed the 11 plus. I was geared to fail at my primary school because I was not selected for special coaching. It was quite an issue at the time and the stigma associated with attending a secondary modern school impacted on relationships with adults and children on the council estate where I lived.

I was assigned to the 'C' stream at eleven which meant that I could not study French. Only those girls in the 'A' and 'B' streams were considered able to cope. It was only later that I became aware of physics and chemistry! I was grateful I was not in the 'E' stream. I enjoyed my school experiences and became fully involved in the work, music and sports on offer. I came near to the top of my class but was held back for two years because I had not studied French. In the third year I moved up and studied French alongside the 'B' streamers – needless to say, progress was limited.

My secondary school had just started to offer CSEs but there were very few girls who stayed on. I was aware of the terrific waste of girls who didn't consider that they were up to further study. They were geared to move into shop or factory work. I had by this stage decided to be a teacher, spurred on from my own experiences and those of my brother who had a poor deal at the boys' secondary modern. I wanted to make a difference. I kept my ambition to myself as I could not be sure whether I was being realistic or how others might react.

I had to transfer to a grammar school to do my sixth form, and I think I had quite a strong sense of 'What is this all about? These people, they're not brain boxes.' It made me feel more strongly about the waste of those who had not felt able intellectually or socially to be able to make that leap. I didn't feel I belonged in the grammar school sixth form. It took two bus journeys to get there and you had to wear a hideous beret. I didn't feel that my needs were particularly addressed in terms of the guidance and support that I got. My involvement in sport was appreciated but I never felt able to continue with my music – I was never asked or encouraged to do so. I didn't feel that I was supported in choosing subjects, or even any guidance as to the next stage. Teacher training college was second place to those who were heading off to university. Nobody suggested that I could go to university first and then train to be a teacher.

Experiences sharpened my insights further. I think the race issue has been brought out, to some extent, by the experiences that my father had when he came to this country after the war from Eastern Europe. His only option was to work on the land. It wasn't till he married my mother, who is English, that it actually gave him a way into work in a factory. To make it easier for those he worked with he became known as 'John' at work. Did it represent a happy compromise or a lack of respect for his cultural identity? He's still not confident as an adult, sensitive about his spoken English. It's safer to retreat – he will still not answer the telephone.

Equal opportunities and social justice have always been a strong reference point in my professional life. I never had a career plan. Each new post presented an opportunity to shape and influence the experiences and life chances of others. Enlisting the support of colleagues, students and parents in creating and developing an accessible, caring and stimulating learning community is always a challenging venture. The journey is both rewarding and frustrating, yet the direction is always clear. Quality assurance activities are an essential feature of a school committed to equal opportunities. Student perceptions and feedback provide a powerful insight, and measure of progress.

An overview of theories of social justice

This section looks at theories of social justice in general, but using the lens of education, from a position of educational activism. Since education is part and parcel of the rest of the social world, social justice in general has a reciprocal relation to social justice in education. One of the most influential theories of social justice, ever, is developed in the context of education: Plato's *Republic*.

Since Plato, there has been no shortage of theories, though most of them barely mention education. Aristotle, though working with Plato's ideas, was more interested in political theory. His conceptualization of social justice in the *Nichomachean Ethics* remains hugely influential on all subsequent Western political philosophy. Rightly so, I think. His formulation is still good. In the later *Politics*, he first explains how individuals come to have a common interest, and then goes on to use the idea to define justice:

> People . . . are drawn together by a common interest, in proportion as each attains a share in the good life. The good life is the chief end both for the community as a whole and for each of us individually.
>
> (Aristotle, *Politics* III, 6, 1278b6)

> The good in the sphere of politics is justice, and justice consists in what tends to promote the common interest.
>
> (Aristotle, *Politics* III, 11, 1282b14)

This he goes on to discuss in terms of distributive justice – the right distribution of benefits in a society. These formulations resonated down the centuries and still do so today.

In contemporary philosophy and political theory, conceptions of social justice are dominated by Rawls, social contract theory and distributive justice – all ideas drawing on a liberal understanding of the legacy of the Enlightenment. Also familiar are other legacies of Enlightenment thinkers, including, for instance, Kant's and Hume's separation of emotion and duty. Some postmodern responses to liberal versions of Enlightenment are influential too. Foremost here are Foucault and Lyotard, both of whom, despite significant theoretical differences between them, have a kind of guarded optimism (or, as Foucault puts it, a hyperactive pessimism) that it is worth struggling for justice. I have said more about this elsewhere (Griffiths 1998a, b). Taylor's and Fraser's discussions of 'recognition' are increasingly familiar, including in educational writing (see, especially, Taylor 1992; Fraser 1997; Gewirtz 1998; Gewirtz and Maguire 2001). A number of other perspectives are widely known: Mouffe's work, which draws on Republican traditions; Michael Walzer's reworking of concepts of distributive justice as 'spheres of justice'; Nussbaum's readings of Plato and Aristotle as going beyond processes of distribution, a position echoed by Iris Marion Young (Walzer 1983; Nussbaum 1986; Young 1990, 2000; Mouffe 1993).

However, philosophy and theory that are contemporary and familiar are just that: it is sobering to note how ideas can be forgotten in just a few decades. There are dissenting or critical – or just different – voices still to be found, despite the loudness of dominant ones. For this reason it is necessary to keep casting about in a critical and thoughtful way, including using works dating from earlier than the previous few years and which may go back decades, even centuries. (I note how few current books on justice mention Hume, even though he is still very much in the mainstream of other philosophical theorizing.) However, there is no need to go back centuries. Runciman (1966), writing less than fifty years ago, is a useful reminder of how much of the moment is the set of references and ideas in the previous paragraph. He discussed Rawls as a new and interesting point of view. Such rediscoveries and reminders are a valuable impetus to thought, preventing theory from ossifying and becoming permanently embedded in an outdated set of examples and contexts.

There are also dissenting ideas to be found in the present. First, there are all the theories from more marginalized thinkers – those uncited and unknown to the mainstream. Feminist and anti-racist work is a major source. (Young and Mouffe are exceptions who have made it in from the margins.) Second, there is another useful source, which may be more likely to represent a wide variety of perspectives. These are to be found in less academic forms of expression, written and otherwise, that address questions of (in)justice but only implicitly theorize it. They include stories, especially personal ones, poems, drama, song, dance and polemic. Jean Barr (1999) points out how much of this work of dissent is necessarily ephemeral. She describes how a dynamic of justice motivated feminist women working in the Workers' Educational Association in the 1970s and 1980s. She points out:

> It was carried out by part-time tutors with little time or resources to write and theorise about their work. Most of the material which emerged from the work was practical, including manuals and tutor workbooks . . . partly remedied by a series of pamphlets produced by the WEA's Women's Advisory Committee during the 1980s.
>
> (Barr 1999: 37)

Third, implicit (and sometimes explicit) theories about justice are to be found in research and development focusing on particular injustices rather than reflecting on them in the abstract: work on gender, environment, race, social class, inclusion, exclusion, SEN and so on (see Dunkwu and Griffiths 2002). All these sources are relevant to any theory claiming to be accountable to those who struggle for justice, as well as to those who theorize it.

It may seem that there are a bewildering number of possibilities. However, if the point of the exercise is kept in mind, then they become helpful rather than bewildering. Accordingly, the point of the exercise is the next topic of discussion: why care about theories?

Prakash Ross. Knowing when to dig in your heels

I don't feel that straight confrontation works as a strategy. However there are times when it is necessary to dig my heels in! In one Local Authority where I worked, my wish to be accepted came unstuck and I got a reputation for being principled and therefore 'can be awkward'. There is also an issue about so-called subversives who are really supporting the status quo.

As a teacher, as a black teacher, I have to prove myself. I have to prove myself as being not just average but better than average. That's a drive in me. When I was appointed as Team Leader for Section 11 in a secondary school, I didn't want to be called the 'Multicultural Department'. I wanted it to be 'Anti-Racist'. I had such a lot of hassle from the teachers! It wasn't *them* that might be upset about it but the *parents* that might be upset about it. Real hassle. 'Multicultural', for me, is steel bands, saris and samosas, that sort of thing. That's how the majority of teachers saw it – as safe. Anti-racism is about challenging the system. It is up-front that you are challenging racism.

I'd been there about three weeks, four weeks, and there was a little group of people who just didn't know how to handle me, didn't know where I was coming from. They were very, very, very careful of me. So I sat in the staff room eating my sandwiches. I always made a point of coming into the staff room and having them. They were talking about a staff hockey match. The Head of Special Needs turned round and said, 'You must be good at hockey. You could be in the team, couldn't you?'

'Why did you say that?' I said.

'Oh, where you come from, you're all good at hockey.'

'Oh? Where do I come from?'

'Oh, India.'

'Well, I come from London,' I said.

'Oh, well, that's near enough.'

It was very funny, or I found it so. I really embarrassed him. But in the end he asked me to come home with him. He learnt from the incident, and, I think, moved on in his thinking.

The trouble with 'social justice' as a term is that it is wishy washy. I have a slight queasiness about the term social justice because it does not imply any professional responsibility to make/move changes. It feels like a moral philosophy, which is OK if others share that concept/belief. Having said this it states, up-front, the particular stance which we all share. Myself, I use 'equality issues'. They are both about a generic fight. It could be about fighting in Chile in the 1970s and Nigeria in the 1990s. It's a very catch-all phrase.

I don't think you can disentangle race. For me as an individual, I can't disentangle race from class, in Britain anyway. I can, as a man, disentangle it from gender, but they are facets of the same. So if I am working on race, I want to say I am working on race. I don't feel as an individual I can fight every fight. I don't want to do that. I think it would just take over, just eat me. If you are committed to something, you can lose yourself as an individual in that commitment. I am not prepared to do that.

Why care about theories?

In getting a theory of social justice, the main question to ask is why anyone might want a theory if they are interested in action: why use theories at all? That is, how might theories of social justice be related to actually doing something practical? The question of how 'theory' relates to 'practice' is vexed and well worn. The following is a brief schematic outline of where different educators and researchers think 'theory' is to be found in relation to 'action'.

- *Theory as something different from action.* This is the classic distinction between *theoria* and *phronesis*: abstract theory about social justice is quite different from the practical wisdom of doing something.
- *Theory into action.* Once there is a theory, what to do will be clear. 'Applied philosophy' assumes this relationship, as does much 'common sense'.
- *A set of rules guiding actions.* This is one example of the previous category, but a particularly influential one.
- *Evidence into theory into actions.* The most well known version of this is 'grounded theory', when it is used for practical purposes.
- *Theory into evidence into theory into action.* Most educational research and development assumes this, as shown by the standard project proposal format, which begins with 'theoretical frameworks' and ends with 'practical outcomes'. However, it also describes some kinds of action research.
- *Experience and action into reflection into action into reflection – in an endless cycle.* This underlies various forms of action research. For some action researchers, the 'reflection' constitutes 'theory', while for others the whole package is 'theory'. Where the 'action' is always understood as 'experience and action', the result may be called 'self-study'.

- *'Action-and-reflection' (or 'Behaviour-and-thought').* This is sometimes referred to as 'theory in action'. Influential versions can be found in Donald Schon's reflective practitioner and Gilbert Ryle's mindful actions (or 'know how') (Ryle 1971; Schon 1983, 1987). It underlies some versions of action research.

This range of possibilities gives rise to a second question. A glance at the list shows that it is not at all obvious what a theory might look like. It can be seen, for instance, that a theory is often taken to be expressed in words, but not always. In some cases, the theory is taken to be inclusive of deeds. In other cases, pictures or diagrams would be good candidates for the theory, as in 'theory into evidence into theory'. 'Reflection' can be expressed in film or dance, as well as in words. Moreover, words themselves are arranged in a range of expressions. A set of rules is one, but only one, possibility. Another possibility would be a set of principles or definitions. Here is a preliminary (corrigible) list of candidates for theory expressible in words:

Principles.
Corrigible principles.
Stories.
Rules.
Corrigible rules.
Descriptions.
Definitions.
Utopias.
Aims.
Objectives.
Performance indicators.
Metaphors.
Political levers.
Strategies.
Praxis.
Genealogy.
Testable hypotheses.
Causal explanations.
Patterns of action.
Dialogues about actions.

The philosophers I mentioned earlier in the chapter express their theories in a range of ways. Plato tells a long reflective story in *The Republic*. Aristotle gives principles. David Hume also gives a story, a compelling and attractive story, but none the less a story, about men and their world (Hume 1740: III ii 2: 225).

'Tis only from the confined generosity of men, along with the scanty provision Nature has made for his wants that justice derives its origins.

He then goes on to derive the idea of justice as rational conventionality. (Is this a persuasive description or a definition?) Rawls, like other social contract theorists, tells a story (about men, about who is to be counted as subject to justice) before putting forward his well known principles. Michael Walzer draws on a number of small-scale stories that help him to give definitions. As he puts it, they are 'Formal definitions that require, as I have tried to show, historical completion' (Walzer 1983: 312).

Philosophers produce theories that are meant to be applicable very generally, even universally. However, as I noted earlier, theorizing about social justice has also come from particular contexts – from work addressing specific circumstances and issues. For instance, there is a lot of theory produced in the course of research and development work addressing specific issues. Most of this work does not produce explicit theory about social justice. The implicit theory has to be abstracted from it. The results of one such attempt are documented in Dunkwu and Griffiths (2002). Some explicit theory may be expressed in ways that do not look like the kinds of theories produced by philosophers or other academics, and so may not even be recognized *as* theory: stories, workbooks, pamphlets, dramatic productions, workshops and so on.

All of the work addressing specific circumstances and issues can be said to constitute an approach that emphasizes diversity, struggle, voice, localized struggles and the claims of the particular and context-bound. They can be called 'little stories' to distinguish them from the 'grand narratives' of universalizing theory (Griffiths 2002). (Alternatively, they might be termed 'modest narratives' as against 'tall tales', in order to change the connotations.) The alternative ways of theorizing or expressing the work's results may include telling personal stories. The work that gives rise to them is most likely to be action research, in the general sense I used above, when listing possible relationships between 'theory' and 'practice'. Personal stories, for instance, such as the ones discussed in Griffiths (2002), are examples of reflection on experience, in order to guide future action. Theory that draws on the personal in its construction and presentation is another example. Barr (1999), from which I quoted earlier, is one such example of theoretical work. She uses her own experiences as a source of theory about living her values as an educator motivated by a dynamic of justice.

I began the chapter by presenting a brief summary of different theories of social justice as found in the standard theory. I went on, in this section, to outline how 'theory' and 'practice' might be related, and mentioned that there are a range of ways of expressing a theory. The next question I consider is how to choose among all these theories. However, this is not an open choice for me. Some of the choices have already been made, as can be seen in how this section, and the book as a whole, has been structured. In particular, the attempt to use both little stories and grand narrative is a continuing thread running throughout. It should be noted, then, that the terms 'grand narrative' and 'little stories' (*petits récits*) are taken from Lyotard, but imply no further debt to him. Instead, the debt is to Richard Smith's (2001) elegant article in which he explores some of the deficiencies of the master narratives of current educational texts.

Betty Kennedy. You don't realize you are being robbed

Probably the education we had up to the age of 11 was good, really very, very good. When we needed to expand there wasn't the opportunity, so you sort of trod water. If you were one of the more intelligent ones in the class, you virtually spent the last couple of years treading water. I spent three years in the top class because by the age of 12 I had done all the curriculum. There were several of us had done. We all sat in this corner against the door and we were given more advanced books and we had to read them ourselves. Then we were set questions on what we had read, in geography, history and English.

We were boosted up to take the scholarship exam at the age of 10. Then you took it again at the age of 11. This was a free scholarship. There was only one place ever given to the school. I was always second in the class. The girl that came first always, she got the scholarship. I nipped back to school one day for some reason when I was 11. I had left a ruler at school or something and I was doing some homework. She was being privately coached by the headmistress. She got it and I didn't. You don't realize at the time you are being robbed. Because when I have seen my children and their friends going on to university, I could have done it easily. I could have gone, but my parents could not afford the three guineas a term to send me. [My friend's] father had a grocery business in the village. Both she and her sister at the age of eleven went to Loughborough Grammar School, because they were paid for. Another girl, her rich uncle paid for her to go to the Nottingham Girls' High. There was nothing like that in our family. There wasn't the money to spare.

I think it was an excellent school. I only wish that the children today were as thoroughly grounded as we were. I think it gave me a jolly good grounding to build on. I have had some responsible jobs. I have brought up four quite well rounded citizens. I have supported a husband and I have looked after a geriatric mother. I think it gave me a jolly firm foundation. Also I have taken a lot of knocks in life as well but I think that education taught me to bounce back. It gave me self-confidence, knowing that I had got ability in certain things. I may not be Einstein but at least I can hold my own with other people. I did feel robbed when it came to my friends learning French. I value the comfortable feeling in that school. The firmness and the fairness. I tell you another thing that was not allowed, that was gangs: 'You can't play with us' etc. So I think it is the firm fairness and the fact that you were expected to do well and to behave yourself and not to do anything that would hurt anybody else either.

A (provisional, unfinished) theory of social justice

It is not obvious where to start in drawing up a theory of social justice that would be useful for educators. The problem for a theorist is that it is relatively easy to draw up a theory for other theoreticians. It is relatively easy, too, to draw up some contexualized theory for a particular small-scale arena of struggle. It is more difficult to do it for a larger area of a particular struggle (for instance, equal opportunities, race, gender). It is very hard indeed to do something theoretical that can bridge the gap between large-scale theory and particular struggles – and that can then be used to do something about injustice. The problem for the non-specialist, the activist, the educator who is trying to do something, is turning particular intuitions and specific theorizing into something that is more general, useful for other circumstances, not getting in the way of other intuitions and actions. Their problems are eased by having a sense of the range of theories possible.

There seem to be so many theories, so many ways of approaching the subject and so many ways of expressing them. Hard-pressed educators might be forgiven for wishing there was only one on offer. However, the rewards of having some knowledge of the range of theories repay the effort of becoming aware of them. Knowing something of the range means that judgements can be made about the uses of any particular theory. It reduces the likelihood of picking a theoretical framework that is unhelpful, even inimical, to the advancement of social justice in any particular context. It also prevents time being wasted. For instance, as I have argued elsewhere, trying to fit school equality policies into a purely liberal framework misses the point of much of what teachers and headteachers are trying to do – and also means that they are less able to defend their good practice against critics (Griffiths 1998b). Meg Maguire and Sharon Gewirtz point out the practical relevance of having the right theory and also show how they can understand each other's points of view all the better for being clear about the frameworks (redistribution and recognition) they are using (Gewirtz and Maguire 2001: 9–10):

> (MM) One of the dilemmas to do with the politics of research and social justice is that 'uncomfortable' things to do with economic inequality have not frequently been dealt with and it's a lot easier to keep them off the agenda.

> (SG) There is a danger associated with the kind of prioritization of

an economic conception of justice that you seem to be advocating, which is that it amounts to an either-or approach. A focus on redistribution is clearly important but ... one of the key aspects of recent theorising about social justice ... is the emphasis on recognition and misrecognition ... Practices which function as mechanisms of disrespect cannot be resolved by a politics of redistribution, but demand a cultural transformation, a shift in the values, language, relationships and structures of schooling.

So far, this chapter has provided a very schematic outline of what the range of theories is, and also of various conceptions of the relationship of theory to practice. The next stage is to begin to make judgements about their use in educational contexts. It is clear that really useful theory is not simply theory done for the pleasure of it, even though such theorizing may well generate useful insights and knowledge. Theory useful for taking action is theory that is intended for use. Equally, theory that is still implicit in practice, rather than explicit, is not yet easy to use. It needs to be made explicit before it can be used in more than a few contexts. The model that seems to be best fitted to the purpose of educational activism is action research, in the sense explained earlier. Certainly, reflection may draw on other forms of theory, from across the range available. It will also draw on personal experience. This description of a focus on action and on personal experience fits well into the newly developing paradigm of research and development known as 'self-study' (Hamilton 2001; Loughran and Russell 2002). It also fits more traditional research and theorizing, if that is translated into action. For instance, Tony Sewell has translated his careful analysis of identity and masculinity in black boys into a number of practical initiatives in schools (Sewell 1997, 2000).

The legitimacy of drawing on the range of theories may be questioned. It may be claimed that wrenching a theory from its core assumptions, 'pearl-fishing', to use Arendt's phrase (Young-Bruehl 1982: 95), is deeply mistaken. In particular, it might be argued that there is a particular problem of using locally developed theories in theorizing justice at all. For it is often claimed that 'social justice', at least as it relates to equality, is a concept that can only be understood within the grand narrative of the Enlightenment and universal claims about reason and rationality. Indeed, it may be argued more generally that any claims about justice are then taken to be true for everyone, everywhere. As Hogan (2001: 8) puts it, in an illuminating discussion of the issue:

The metaphysical aim of seeking an understanding of justice which has freed itself for subjective perspectives and from the intrigues of powerful interest groups is an attractive one ... It would be a concept that is universally applicable.

This would appear to leave no space for the little stories (modest narratives) and local theories that make no claim to be true for all people at all times. Onora O'Neill (1996) provides a useful overview of both these positions. She also makes a persuasive argument that such extreme claims are misleading, in that they falsely and unhelpfully conflate focus with scope: that a principle has a universal focus does not imply that it also has a cosmopolitan scope. Her argument implies that we need to stop polarizing claims of structure and context and find ways of understanding their interrelationship.[1] The small-scale has to cohere with the large-scale, and be understood in relationship with it.

One way of understanding the relationship between the small- and large-scale is that it is dynamic. Thus any theory is never the last word, but always corrigible, always revisable. Thus, a large-scale theory can be put into question by the perspectives of a little story. Indeed, it is likely that this will happen, as contexts change. Walzer's remark that 'definitions need historical completion' can be understood in this light. For instance, I quoted Aristotle approvingly. But it is clear that my understanding, in the twenty-first century, with the little stories available to me, of 'the common interest', 'the good life' or 'the community' would be very different from his, in ancient Greece, impressed, as he was, by the little stories of Athenian gentlemen. However, to argue for a due humility about the uncertainty of any theory is nothing new. Hogan (2001: 20) argues that Socrates (unlike Plato) exemplified the continual search for uncertain, unfinished understandings:

> He devoted his life's work to this search but he also slowly discovered and continually warned by his own example, that it was a serious illusion to think that any human could arrive at the final goal, or that humans could assume a God's eye view of all of reality ... What justice in educational practice might properly look like begins to emerge from reflection on lessons such as these. Its most promising sources lie in ... something intimately concerned with the unfinishing character of learning itself.

Finally, having settled on the kind of theory that is wanted, it is important that whatever theory is developed is coherent with other philosophical judgements, particularly those related to theories of self, of relationship, of speech and action, of the good and of the right, private and public and so on. That is, whatever particular theory is judged useful, and whatever pearls have been fished, the result has to fit with the overall theoretical-practical positions underlying actions.

In the course of the three chapters of Part 1, I have been establishing various theoretical commitments. They are: (a) the need for both 'grand narratives' and 'little stories' (which exist in relation to the other) in any understanding of social justice; (b) the necessity of any theory being assumed to be dynamic, i.e. corrigible and responsive to new perspectives and changing contexts; (c) the view that the self is constructed in and against relationship with various social groupings, which are themselves constructed by relationships with individual selves; (d) an acknowledgement of the dual significance of material resources and of cultural identity, i.e. of both 'culture' and 'structure', of both 'redistribution' and 'recognition'; (e) the view that social groupings are not fixed, but are in a continuous process of construction, of changing, of shifting. Moreover, different social groupings intersect with each other.

These commitments together can be used to develop Aristotle's insight that social justice is to be found in the good of both individual and the society as a whole. The result will be one that he would not accept at all! Here is how I express it. Social justice is a dynamic state of affairs that is good for the common interest, where that is taken to include both the good of each and the good of all, in an acknowledgement that one depends on the other. The good depends on mutual recognition and respect and also on a right distribution of benefits and responsibilities. It includes paying attention to individual perspectives at the same time as dealing with issues of discrimination, exclusions and recognition, especially on the grounds of (any or all of) race, gender, sexuality, special needs and social class. It is dynamic in that it is never – could never be – achieved once and for all. So getting it is a matter of resolving possible tensions about the well-being of individuals, of whole societies and of social political groups.

Finally, since all this is corrigible, it is tentative theorizing. The idea is well expressed by Jean Rath. She displays (asks us to display) a proper delicacy and caution (particularly about policing the boundaries of 'social justice') at the same time as acting on a desire to do more than sit fretting in an armchair (Rath 2000):

> We can make no attempt to formulate transcendent rules for the shackling of practices to 'theoretical frameworks' . . . Everything is kept in motion through the recognition of the constant need to reiterate the question 'Where do you draw the fine line between "anything goes" and "anything may go" (when nothing basic is taken for granted)?' (Trinh 1992: 259)

Note

1 O'Neill (1996: 4) writes: 'A focus on universal principles cannot fix the *scope of ethical consideration*: it cannot show *who* falls within the domain of universal principles. Universality is in the first instance only the formal property of holding for all rather than only for some cases within a specified domain' (italics in the original).

4 Social justice in education: a framework

Introduction

At the end of Chapter 3 I gave a statement about how social justice can be understood. It expressed a number of discrete but related arguments:

1 Social justice is a verb; that is, it is a dynamic state of affairs in that it is never – could never be – achieved once and for all. It is always subject to revision.
2 The good for each person both affects and depends on the good for all – where 'all' can be understood as being small face-to-face groups, structural groups (constructed both by positioning and by self-identification) and the society as a whole. How these groupings are made up is never fixed.
3 Social justice depends on both 'recognition' and 'redistribution'.
4 The issues need to be understood in terms both of 'little stories' and of 'grand narratives'; that is, both localized issues and large-scale theorizing about them.

The statement was not focused particularly on education. In this chapter, I develop a framework for active approaches to social justice in education.

Sharon Baillon. I just hated it altogether

It was boring. All of it. Teachers, talking. I would go in, head for the back of the class and think, 'Oh, don't pick on me! I don't know! Don't pick on me!' I would sit there writing my name on the table – just to look as if you were doing what you were meant to be doing. You used to copy each other's work. I would never have got through if I didn't – I just hated it so much. You go to school because you have got to and you have got to do it. You are either into it or you are not.

Homework was never done on time, always late. I used to think 'I have had enough of this at school without coming home and doing it.'

I wasn't disruptive or really naughty. I just used to not want to be noticed. I'd go straight to the back of the room and get as far away as I could and just think, 'Don't ask me! Don't ask me!' My mind used to wander. I would look through the window, and then: 'Sharon, what's line 4 say?'

'Line 4? Line 4 on which page?' I'd say.

I was 10 pages behind. I'd get shown up then, wouldn't I? Because I wasn't following.

When we had cross-country, I didn't used to do that. I only used to live across the road from school and there used to be a group of us. We'd break from the start, double back a few steps, wait till they had gone and we used to go and sit in my house until they came round by where I lived. Then we joined back in and said we had done the whole lot. We hadn't. It was about the only exciting bit really.

Oh, I really hated the needlecraft, as it was called. 'Sharon, you don't thread the cotton like that on the machine,' she used to say. I used to think, 'Well, you do it then.' She used to have these bright red nails – I can see them shining at me now – and thick red lipstick and big glasses. We had to make an apron and a blouse with a Peter Pan collar. I never did finish either of them.

I can remember dissecting a rat. Well, we were supposed to, but I couldn't do it. The rat was just part of your science lesson. Just all pinned on the board and then you were supposed to cut it down the middle. 'I can't do that,' I said. I walked out the class. There were three of us. I think they just said: 'If you can't do it, you can't do it.' I used to like science, actually, I suppose because we used to mess about. We used to put things on the gas taps and mess about with Bunsen burners.

I can remember my first day at school. I can remember my teacher saying: 'What are you crying for?' I remember walking across the playground and seeing my mum disappearing around the corner to go to work. There was nothing she could do because she had got to go – and that's it. My mum couldn't do a lot about me not liking it at school. She was on her own. She had got to go to work. So that was it. I had got to go to school. 'Well why don't you like it?' she used to say. 'I just don't like it because it's boring. I would rather stay at home,' I used to say. 'But you can't. You have to go to school.'

All I wanted was a job with some money. I was 16 when I left. I felt absolutely brilliant when I left because I had already got a job. I was waiting until after my sixteenth birthday. I worked in a paintbrush factory, sorting paintbrushes. We used to have quite a good laugh. It was not bad at all. The money was good. That was all I wanted.

I do regret it now. I look back sometimes and I think, I should have tried harder. When you look at what you are doing, you think you should have tried.

I want my daughter to enjoy school, not be like I used to be, upset in the morning. I used to think, 'Oh no! I have got to go to school again.' I don't want her to feel like that. I just want her to go because she wants to go and enjoy what she is doing, which (touch wood!) she has done up to now. She's nearly 16. Sixteen in September.

Starting assumptions and guiding principles

In this chapter, I develop a framework that is intended to be widely applicable throughout education. It is developed within a British context, but should apply to other Western countries. It should apply across all phases: nursery, primary, secondary, tertiary, post-compulsory, informal. Within those phases it should apply to people working at all levels: classroom; school, college, university; local government; central government. Some of it should also apply to more informal learning in community organizations. Inevitably, the framework is quite general. In Part 2, I explore how the general framework might apply in specific contexts.

There are important principles about education that influence what might count as social justice, as was explained in Chapter 1. Education is about learning. Sometimes it is also about teaching. It has always been valued for two things, which are sometimes in tension with each other. First, it is a good in itself. Second, it is a competition for glittering prizes and a means of opening the doors to privilege. Learning that is good in itself is marked by human relationships, which include fun, love, laughter, tears, obsessions. For education is always about people. They appear in various roles: children, teachers, teacher educators, policy makers, researchers, governors, parents, inspectors. Like all human beings they are marked by their socio-political positionings, whether or not they acknowledge such positioning as part of their identity: race, class, gender, religion, sexuality, disability, severe learning difficulties, emotional and behavioural difficulties, nationality, ethnicity and so on. These positionings influence who wins, who loses, and who gets what they want as a result of their involvement with education.

In Chapter 2, I remarked on the damaging effects of trying to smooth out differences, of making people choose between being a 'parvenu' or a 'pariah' (Arendt 1973). I argued that if people are to benefit from their education, it is important for them to have a say and have their say heard. This means making space for a wide range of expression: for stories, music and polemical outbursts as well as for academic 'plain prose'. I further argued that for education to be of benefit to all, we would all have to learn to have our say within a kind of 'transversal politics' (Cockburn and Hunter 1999). This politics, like social justice, is a verb. It is always unfinished, always revisable.

Eulalee Brown. Scope to thrive

I am from a very stable background with a very supportive and extensive family network. My family, during my childhood in Jamaica, instilled in me strong principles, reinforced the idea that I was valued, and that it was possible to achieve the highest standards in any endeavour. It is because of these principles that I was able to survive within the stereotyping and racist environment that existed within the education establishment of the Yorkshire Dales, where I undertook my primary and secondary education.

After leaving school, I moved to Birmingham to reside within a community that would reflect my ethnic background. This provided me with a safe and secure environment where there was scope for me, as a black woman, to thrive.

The Harambee Organisation provided me with my first job as a clerical worker. I was subsequently promoted to running the book and African arts shop. Harambee expanded its services to include a housing association and the Marcus Garvey Nursery. The nursery was a black educational establishment providing African Caribbean children with a safe, stable and protective environment where they were able to express themselves, explore their heritage, learn about their culture and develop their fullest potential. There were no negative racial stereotypes to hinder their education.

As a young mother who had strong political beliefs in the equality of opportunities for people of colour, the Organisation reinforced my outlook, which I also found to be beneficial to my child. My daughter was one of the first intake of this well needed project. During the period that she attended I was roped in to assist with the catering. Although I couldn't cook I was prepared to learn. When asked to 'shred the cabbage' I was taken aback. Fortunately, another worker whispered and motioned to me to use a knife to cut it into fine strips. The manager, thinking I could cook, offered me the job. Within months, I was made a nursery assistant, as my relationship with the children was noticed. I remained in this post for two years. I then got married, had my second child, and when he was 18 months old, returned to college to further my education.

During my time at the nursery, I found it a very supportive network for all members of the black community. My children and I benefited tremendously from the services provided by the Organisation, but it was my family values which always reminded me to reach for my goals.

I am now a qualified social worker with over 20 years' experience in the field of childcare, with a BSc honours degree and other qualifications gained throughout my career. My daughter is a qualified primary school teacher, my first son is a computer and sound engineer, working within the music industry, and my second son who also benefited from the Marcus Garvey Nursery is doing very well at primary school, in the top set for all subjects. I have always maintained my links with the local community and given my services on a voluntary basis when required.

A framework for social justice in education

As I have shown, both social justice and education are extremely complicated to understand and work with. It is no wonder that the overall practical situation is too fragmented for anyone to keep in mind all the time. If anyone were to attempt it, they would surely get it wrong, given its complex intercon- nections, its many levels, its unknowns. Indeed, it could be thought arrogant of anyone to work on the assumption that they could know for each learner what is being learned and how that feels, especially in terms of their developing identity.

No teacher is in any position to decide what aspects of a learner's identity are significant. Each generation of learners (be they children or adults) has to work out its own accommodations with positioning by race, class and gender in the contemporary context (this is what Arendt 1958 calls 'natality'). Think of Jennifer and Edwin Maxwell (Chapters 1 and 2). Each of them arrived in Nottingham from Jamaica, as children. Looking back to my own teaching experience as a young teacher in the 1970s, the best I can say is that at least I knew that I did not know very much about the perspectives of the British Jamaican children I taught. (Though I did see that their parents were puzzled as well. They, of course would have been making their own accommodations. I also saw that a Jamaican colleague was puzzled, too.) Ghazala Bhatti's sensitive learning histories of her own students (see Chapter 6, and also Bhatti 2001) are further evidence that it would be impossible for anyone but the learners them- selves to work with the contradictory categories that mark each one of them (us). How can we hope to know what is going on now for, say, mixed-race children, asylum seekers and Eastern Europeans – even if we fall into one or more of those categories ourselves. How might we advise individual Jewish young people and their Muslim (possibly Arab) classmates, as they react to news of conflicts in the Middle East – even if, especially if, we fall into one of those categories ourselves.

Luckily, the conclusion of the arguments of Part 1 of the book is that no teacher (or policy maker, manager or school governor) need worry that they cannot know everything about learners. A better strategy is (a) to listen and talk and then, further, (b) to consult and cooperate in order (c) to take action. With luck and hard work, it may be possible (d) to act together as a collective. These activities depend on (e) respecting and valuing both ourselves and others. All this is rewarding, even though very hard. This can usefully be expressed as a cycle with arrows going both ways (Figure 4.1).

There is always a danger with human relationships that difficulties are avoided rather than confronted. Listening, talking, consultation, cooperation, respect and value accorded to people: all this sounds pleasant, even cosy. But it is far from it. Working for social justice is never cosy! Anyone who thinks that it is needs to pay attention to Robin Richardson's warning that there will be argument and tears (Richardson 1989; see quotation in Chapter 7). There is a particular danger that some aspects of social justice work might seem too dif- ficult to confront, too likely to provoke discomfort. It is all too easy to avoid those areas in favour of continuing to work on something easier. Therefore,

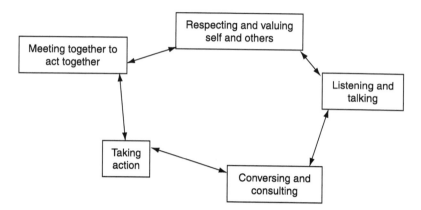

Figure 4.1 A model of action for social justice in education

there is a need to exercise constant vigilance, together with a continuing willingness to dream the impossible. One way of doing this is regularly to ask some difficult, challenging questions about what is being done. This process might usefully be thought of as a self-audit, which makes use not of the easy FAQs ('frequently asked questions'), but of QAFs ('questions to ask frequently'). QAFs might include:

- 'Who is benefiting?'
- 'Who is not benefiting?'
- 'What do they think about it?'
- 'What do they feel about it?'
- 'Are men, women, white people, black people, working-class people (and so on) represented in person in a specific grouping such as a student body, staff body, conference, exam board, government advice panel?'
- 'Are they represented in the curriculum?'

And, most importantly:

- 'How do we know the answers to those questions?'
- 'What evidence is there?'

This framework is very general and schematic. It has been used to structure Part 2, where more specific concerns and contexts are addressed. An even more general 'take home message' is in Chapter 10, along with a warning that any exercise of this kind – trying to pin down social justice – is always unfinished business.

PART 2
A Framework for Social Justice in Schools and Colleges

5 Self-esteem: ordinary differences and the difference they make

Introduction

I was still in my teens when I learnt that self-esteem was connected with social justice. Martin Luther King was to preach in St Paul's Cathedral, and I was fortunate enough to be there to hear his sermon – somehow my mother had got tickets for the two of us. He preached a sermon on the text 'Love thy neighbour as thyself'. I had expected yet another exhortation to unselfishness. Instead I heard him explain that unless you loved yourself, you could not love your neighbour – and vice versa. He explained that it was hard for many black people in the United States to love themselves and they had to learn to do so. It was a sermon I still remember nearly half a century later, and it is part of the theme of this chapter, and this book. So this chapter is about respecting and valuing oneself and others: about what is usually referred to as 'self-esteem'. (To put this another way, and using a term borrowed from the black culture of the United States, it is also about getting an attitude, and valuing it in others.)

Over the years, in the course of a number of research projects, I have conducted interviews and had conversations with people who have related their life stories to issues of social justice. Again and again, the issue of self-esteem has come up in relation not to achievement but to being made to feel peculiar, inferior, ashamed. Stories were told: of being singled out for being black, of the relief of finding that other gay/bisexual educators existed, of the effect of having a migrant father, as Jennifer's story (Chapter 1) and Nada's story (Chapter 3) show. I recall stories from Nottingham primary schools (Griffiths and Davies 1995): the distressing story of Tom, a boy teased for his lesbian mother, and the poignant relief and pleasure of the isolated black child in a white suburban school when a visiting African teacher volunteered to assist in his classroom for a term. Likewise, many of the stories woven into this book show how respecting and valuing oneself and others is central to recognizing, getting and struggling for justice.

Self-esteem: individualism, achievement and zero-sum games

(This section draws extensively on an article written jointly with Deborah Chetcuti (Chetcuti and Griffiths 2002).)

We begin by articulating some of the assumptions about self-esteem that underlie much of the psychological and social psychological educational theory about it. The idea of self-esteem has a long history. It has come into education through the work of psychologists and social psychologists, especially through the work of James (1892), Cooley (1902), Mead (1934), Coopersmith (1967), Burns (1979) and Rogers (1983). (See overviews in Lawrence 1987; Renshaw 1990; Griffiths 1993.) This history strongly colours current orthodoxy about self-esteem. Briefly, this is as follows.

First, self-esteem is to be understood in terms of individuals and their face-to-face relationships. Second, it can be treated as an independent variable and measured in relation to achievement (does it correlate with high achievements?) or social groups (does it vary by gender, ethnicity, social class and so on?). Causal relations can then be discovered. Third, more is always better. This orthodoxy in the theoretical literature is highly significant because it is congruent with the orthodoxy to be found in practice. Books on classroom practice focus on individual responses and face-to-face relationships. Many of them suggest that enhancing self-esteem will improve achievement (or vice versa), especially for disadvantaged groups, and that improving it is always a good thing. Examples can be found across the English-speaking world. In the UK, examples include Lawrence (1987), Wetton and Cansell (1993) and Roberts (1995). See Kenway and Willis (1990) for an overview of Australian programmes. Finally, Borda and Borda (1978), Pope *et al.* (1988) and Thompson and Lowson (1995) are examples of the long history of interest in self-esteem in North American schools.

We go on to summarize the nature of the critique of that individualistic approach, and to indicate alternatives. The thought of criticizing the orthodoxies of self-esteem is very strange to many educators. As Kenway (1990) puts it, to be critical of them can seem close to being critical of happiness. But, like her, we think it important to critique and reconstruct them, because they can be dangerously narrow, skewing efforts to improve efforts to help children value themselves while valuing others.

First, while individual responses and face-to-face relationships are crucial to self-esteem, an image of oneself is not formed in a social or cultural vacuum. As Kenway and Willis argue, since the discourse of self-esteem is individualistic it ignores the asymmetrical relations of power within which cultures operate. So it directs attention away from the struggle for justice, in which the distribution of power is all-important. They argue (Kenway and Willis 1990: 42):

> What this means is that those features of the education system which sift, sort, grade, classify and, in the process, distribute and attribute value and valuelessness are not confronted . . . Clearly schools don't (can't, won't) allow all students to be 'successes'. This discourse almost seeks to 'gentle the masses' into feeling good about failure.

The self itself is formed by how it responds to being 'thrown' (to use a Heideggerean term) into the world in a particular material, social and political context (Griffiths 1995). Each person responds in her own way to the world, and articulates her own perceptions, ideas and purposes. Operating, as she must, within the power structures of that world, she works out her ideas and purposes, within the givenness of her being a child, a boy or a girl, a man or woman, rich or poor, Jewish, Muslim, Christian or entirely secular. So each person can, as Arendt helpfully says, 'make articulate and call into full existence what otherwise they would have to suffer passively anyhow' (Arendt 1958: 208). So self-esteem is developed in relation to both intimate and political groups over lifetimes which begin in babyhood and go through the changes of adulthood.

Second, the attempt to treat achievement and socio-political groups as independent variables in relation to self-esteem ignores how the self has been constructed in relation to those groups and, further, how socio-political structures are implicated in what counts as 'successful achievement' (Renshaw 1990; Griffiths 1993, 1995; Bredo 1999). The danger of this individualist approach is that it ignores the systematic influences of power relations in a society. It encourages a deficit approach, which blames those with lower self-esteem for their lacks and failings. For the proponents of such an approach, if any 'underclass' lacks self-esteem, compensatory programmes can be devised which need not address its socio-economic and political position.

The individualistic approach is simplistic. True, we are individual human beings with our individual strengths and failings, but to be human is to have social relationships that affect our sense of self. Part of constructing oneself as a person is to judge oneself against standards of achievement and performance. Those standards can be set by the individual herself, or for her by peers, parents, teachers, newspapers, celebrities and so forth. Not surprisingly, if a person wants to identify with two groups that seem to impose different conditions of entry, it will be difficult for her to attain a robust sense of self-esteem. This situation is exacerbated if she has to prove herself worthy of acceptance in a group through evidence of adequate achievement and performance. That is, she is forced into a situation in which she thinks, 'If what I do is good enough, I will be loved and valued by this group that I value and want to love.' Contrast this with the happier thought: 'I am loved and valued by this group, so what I do is good, and I will do the best I can at it.'[1]

Third, the assumption that more self-esteem is always better seems to have become widespread in educational discourse. It seems hard even to question this idea within education (as evidenced by the stir caused by a recent study that did so: Emler 2001). However, there are clues in our ordinary language to how other points of view endure. It may seem that the language of self-esteem has drowned out other related terms, such as pride, arrogance, confidence, self-respect and humility. But these concepts are not so easily by-passed. They remain embedded in everyday talk. Indeed, they are forcibly and colourfully expressed in everyday English. One person may say of another that she is full of herself, thinks too much of herself, puts people down to make herself seem big. Australians talk of the tall poppy. The English speak of stuck-up snobs.

It is important to question the assumption that 'more is better'. There are significant cases where it is not. In particular, there is the widespread behaviour based on the assumption that a person can enhance her self-esteem by asserting herself to be better than someone else. The assertion need not be related to any particular achievement or performance: the assertion can be made by using pejoratives related to race, class, sexuality, gender, disability . . . The list of people vulnerable to this kind of insult seems endless. Think of the death in the playground of the popular, confident, high achiever, 13-year-old Ahmed Ullah, at the hands of friendless, underachieving, 13-year-old Darren Coulson, who sneered 'Paki' as he drove home the fatal knife. It seems that he tried to gain self-esteem from being white (MacDonald 1990). The same seems to be true for Stephen Lawrence's murderers. Such an assumption depends on believing that the distribution of self-esteem is a zero-sum game: more for one person means less for someone else. This is at the heart of the reason why self-esteem is an issue of social justice. Any approach that assumes the more an individual's self-esteem the better makes it hard to see, let alone criticize, these zero-sum games of self-esteem in which a person builds herself up by despising others.

We suggest that the difference between such zero-sum games and a productivity of self-esteem can be captured by the difference between the concepts of 'arrogance' and 'self-respect'. Arrogance is maintained by a person feeling they are in competition with others, and winning. Self-respect, on the other hand, depends for its maintenance on wanting everyone else to have it too. The use of pejoratives is an example of the way one person's enhanced self-esteem becomes another person's put-down; how arrogance may be a substitute for self-respect. Schooling cannot escape being a competition. But it need not be an all-encompassing, zero-sum game. Some discourses of difference need to be reconstructed if this is to work. These discourses are, especially, the oppressive ones where some children are defined as not what the relatively powerful are: masculine, posh and so on. They also include those reactive discourses where the relatively oppressed sneer at the attributes of their oppressors.[2]

Ordinary differences

In the previous section, a finger of blame was pointed at zero-sum games for the tendency for people to build on arrogance rather than on self-respect for their self-esteem. And it was also pointed at the culture of individualism for the necessary, but dangerously insufficient, response to that tendency in terms of personal, face-to-face acceptance and liking. One particularly serious example is the conflation of harassment (defined as attempted intimidation on the grounds of race, sex, disability, sexuality and so on) with bullying (defined as attempted intimidation of one individual by another). Schools and researchers alike are all too likely to dismiss name-calling as less serious than other forms of bullying, regardless of whether the name-calling is harassment or not. The seriousness of harassment is of a different order – not in terms of its immediate effect on the individuals directly concerned, but in terms of the long-term effect on the whole set of people who are applauded or disparaged by association.

If there is to be a move beyond zero-sum games and the individualism that is an inadequate response to them, then there must be an alternative way of understanding difference. This is precisely what has proved to be so difficult in practice. On the one hand, the assertion of the significance of difference can lead to a strengthening of stereotypes. On the other, the assertion of the commonality of people can lead to a denial of the significance of social and political difference. Faced with racism displayed by the likes of Darren Coulsen it is too easy *either* to condemn him as an example of disaffected racist, white, working-class youth, *or* to see him as a victim of extraordinarily difficult personal circumstances. Both are true, and this is what proves so difficult to deal with, practically – as the MacDonald inquiry into the murder showed – and theoretically. Indeed, the tension between the two positions is one of the main threads of inquiry running through this book.

Why should it be so difficult to deal with differences? Why is there such a tendency to think either in stereotypes, as if any human being could be defined only in terms of their biology or background, or in strictly individual terms, as if human beings were not social, political creatures? That there is a difficulty is obvious. Why it should exist is not. It is possible that the problem lies with a certain fixation, at least in the culture of the West, on dualist categories, as feminists have long argued. It is possible that the problem also lies with the success of abstraction and simplification in some areas of knowledge, so that it can seem that the fewer dimensions needed for understanding a situation, the better it will be controlled.

Whatever the reason why the issue is so difficult, it is necessary to find a better way of dealing with it. Perhaps some bewilderment that the issue is difficult is a good place to start. Difference is ordinary. We all know from all our everyday experiences that human beings are not defined only in terms of their biology or background. Equally, we are well aware that we and everyone we meet are social, political creatures and we are well aware of the importance to most people of gender, ethnic background, class and religion, even if we do not hold them to be important ourselves.

Ordinary differences are inescapable in schools and classrooms. Education, like any human undertaking, is a process that encounters a various and diverse cast of characters: teachers, learners, policy makers, parents, administrators, support staff and advisors who are different personally, socially, politically, biologically, sexually, historically, ethnically, physically – as well as being different precisely because they are teachers, learners, policy makers, parents, administrators, support staff or advisors. Differences due to sex, race, class, ability to pass tests and so on are normal and form part of the everyday life of classrooms, as do differences of religion, skin colour or an ear for music. As do differences of eye colour, height, taste in clothes, foot measurement, blood group, tidiness and a liking for sweet things. These are not differences from a norm: the existence of difference is normal. There is no norm.[3]

Some observations from Hannah Arendt are very useful here (see also Chapter 2). She points out that no system can eliminate difference, the attempt to do so is self-delusion and the result, if it could be successful (the dream of totalitarianism), would be petrifaction (see quotation in Chapter 1). The dream of equality that pushes difference into the private realm reduces everyone to being the same. Worse, any person who asserts a difference runs the risk of being defined by that and that only (Arendt 1973: 302):

> If a Negro in a white community is considered a Negro and nothing else, he loses along with his right to equality that freedom of action which is specifically human; all his deeds are now explained as 'necessary' consequences of some 'Negro' qualities; he has become some specimen of an animal species, called man.

She developed the useful concept of 'the exception Jew' (or as she called herself once, though she was no feminist, an 'exception woman'), which is very helpful for understanding how an ideology of sameness works, by granting 'exception' status to some members who deviate from 'the norm'. The possibility of being an exception also helps to keep social control. In education, this is especially obvious in relation to class. Surely the chance of some social mobility gives the examination system its power even when many in the population are cynical about the way the system works to benefit the rich.

The complexity of all this would be hard to exaggerate. Hannah Arendt herself provides a useful example. In her youth, between the two world wars, she studied philosophy, and thought of herself as part of the German intellectual tradition. But as she remarked, once the Nazis became powerful, 'If one is attacked as a Jew, one must defend oneself *as a Jew*' (Young-Bruehl 1982: 109). She was also a migrant, a refugee/asylum seeker and a learner of English as a second language. She was white, highly educated, clever, able-bodied and middle class. More personal characteristics can be gleaned from her biographer: she liked mountains, she was a loyal friend, she had to mediate the difficult relation between her mother and husband, she disliked taking part in street demonstrations and so on. It is hard to say how much of all this is significant in relation to her philosophy and other writing. It is plainly relevant that she was Jewish. On the other hand, she was keen to distance herself from feminism, yet she is often discussed by commentators precisely because she is a woman (one of the very few to make it into the canon of standard philosophy courses). And it is hard to imagine that her experience as a refugee/asylum seeker was irrelevant to her writing about the human rights of displaced persons. What is evident in all this is that there is no single axis of difference. Nor is there a hierarchy of difference, such that, for instance, her identification as a philosopher or her cleverness is more or less important than her identification as a Jew, her position as a woman or her loyalty. Her education affected all of these characteristics. And all of them are more or less important only in relation to particular issues. For her, as a human being, all of them matter.

Complexity is not necessarily chaotic or anarchic. There are systematic differences and similarities among the various kinds of characteristics. First, some of them are differences of individual temperament and talent. Mozart had an exceptional talent for music, as Archimedes had for mathematics. Some people find tunes hard to hold, and others find it difficult to grasp the pleasures of number and geometry. Second, some differences are material. That is, they are caused by the arrangements of society, such as relative riches and poverty, or caused by physical states of the body, such as being blessed with good vision and hearing or, alternatively, having short sight and deafness. These differences have clear educational consequences, unless particular actions are taken. (Think of free libraries and museums or privileged, private schools. Think of the significance of being able to use glasses and of having good lighting in schools. Think of the difference a deaf loop can make.) Some differences would not have educational consequences if society did not make such a big deal of them. These are differences such as those of sexuality, sex, race and religion. But society does make a big deal of them; and so the arguments related to recognition and respect as part of social justice are highly relevant to education (see Part 1).

Educators need to develop ways in which differences can be taken for granted and, where they get in the way of learning, how they can be compensated for. (This may be as easy as wearing spectacles. It may be a question of recognizing that only some people are straight, white, middle class, and having that recognition embedded in the curriculum.) We also need to re-examine how differences are constructed by social structures such as schools themselves, which constrain students to develop a sense of self based only on their success (or failure) in examinations. We need to think about a way in which differences can be discursively reconstructed to take into account all differences and celebrate their existence – that is, celebrate the wonderful diversity of humanity – rather than make difference merely something to be tolerated. This acceptance of difference will allow students to believe in themselves as they are, with all their diverse talents and characteristics, and this will really allow them to develop their full potential and their authentic identity. This would require attention to the myriad axes of difference and also to making sure that there were no pernicious group putdowns.

Getting real: a different education

Each chapter in Part 2 has a section called 'Getting real'. The purpose is to move from an examination of ideas in general terms – where examples are used to illuminate the theorizing – to a more practical perspective. It is also important to see what practical use can be made of the ideas in specific circumstances: for *real individuals*, with their *specific socio-political positions* (race, class, gender, sexuality and so on), in *particular educational contexts* (classrooms, schools, tertiary institutions) and *in relation to identifiable communities* (their own members, local communities, advisers, universities, national or international networks of educators). This section is not intended to give lots of tips for lessons or policies. Instead, it is intended to inspire and illuminate, by showing the ideas in action, in all their contextual specificity, enacted by real people. It is hoped that these examples will help educators to rethink what they, themselves, might do in their own contexts.

Learning to mix with anyone and everyone

Jacky speaks as the class teacher in a primary school in the city centre. She herself is of African-Caribbean heritage. (At the time she spoke, she was deputy head of the school, as well as being class teacher. Since then, she has become headteacher of another city-centre school.) She talked of teaching children to value themselves without feeling they had to put down others to do it. When someone has 'an advantage', it is one that would be enhanced if others shared it.

These children from our school can mix with a variety of people from so many different backgrounds that they are at an advantage. When they go to places like [the local elite schools] the people there are the ones that are frightened. They are at a disadvantage because they cannot mix with our children. Whereas our children can mix with them and more. I've got kids that have been going for the exams [to enter one of the elite local schools]. One of them was saying to me, 'Well, when we were there, we were lining up, there were people there who were very nervous. They were looking at me. I was the only black person.' 'Well you shouldn't feel nervous about that,' I said. 'Oh, no, I wasn't, but my Mum was,' she said. 'I'm glad you weren't. Don't let that put you off, or anything like that. Imagine how those people feel,' I said. 'They're the ones at a disadvantage, because they're the ones who are frightened of you! You shouldn't be frightened of them. You can mix with anyone!'

What I'm looking for in a good school is a school where people can feel valued for whatever things that they can contribute to the school, and where people feel comfortable about being in that school, and feel they can be themselves. So they don't have to hide what they eat. Or they can't talk about certain things because someone's going to pick on them. I want people to feel comfortable about the way they dress if they wear the dreadlocks, or if they wear their hair in wraps, or whatever.

The aims of education of black children in a black community nursery

Melrose used to be the head of the Marcus Garvey black community nursery that Syble helped to start (see Chapter 2). She is proud of the level of achievement of its pupils: 'Sometimes the teachers at the first schools couldn't believe it when parents went in and said, "My child can read and write already".' She explains its ethos of respect and self-respect and how it was achieved.

None were allowed to fail. Even if they weren't able to do the alphabet, they were able to do something. We looked at the individual child and what they were good at and tried to develop that, because not all children are academically minded. So in that sense, even if it was just to get the children to socialize, that is something. It wasn't all about they must do this, they must do that. It was sometimes just about the children being able to play with one another.

We had a lot of support from the parents who would come in and give their time free, to assist with the children, to listen to them reading, doing simple number work, or building things. Quite a few parents did that.

It is also about children seeing black people in a positive way. Mixing with other black people and enjoying being with other black people. Sometimes you send them to a city council nursery and all they see are white people in positions of authority. Again, when they go to school, this is also the norm. You are not actually teaching them what they can achieve; but to see people of the same colour, doing things with them that they are also going to do when they get to school is quite something.

We tried to instil in the children they can be as good as they want to be rather than comparing them with a white person. It's for them to go out there and do the best they can rather than look at that person.

From social isolation to social inclusion

Elizabeth[4] is the deputy head of a rural grammar school, with a reputation for high academic achievement. She explains how the school deals with some issues of social exclusion that are not easily reduced to issues such as social class or (dis)ability, but that nevertheless have their roots in socio-political structures. The aim is to move to help pupils to respect difference in each other, and gain self-respect in the process.

Another problem, which has surfaced more and more in the last year or two, and that is a social isolation problem within a group. It's not the government's social isolation problem. We've had a few weirdos in the school, partly because we tend to get some people who are very bright and who've got a very narrow range of experience, I suppose. Partly because a lot of them live in very isolated communities, farms or out in the fens or whatever. The only point of contact is the television and the computer. We also have some very old-fashioned parents who have what I think are quite strange ideas. This doesn't help their children to socialize. We've got one or two oddballs, eccentrics who are absolutely great – but they are eccentrics. Mostly the school likes eccentrics, the staff particularly. A lot of the kids are quite happy with them. But over the last two years, we do seem to have had a number of social misfits for various reasons.

The teacher will say, 'Get into pairs!' And there's the odd one left out at the end. It's taken several years to try and get to the stage with the staff of, 'You organize the groups and the pairs. Don't let the kids do it themselves.' That was one of the things we wanted to work on, to say we'll get a balance between classwork, group work and individual work, and we will move people round. The teacher must insist that they work in groups to try and prevent social exclusion.

It's been the people who are considered the swots, the nerds, quote. We have tried to tackle it pastorally when there's a problem, obviously. But teacher grouping is a preventative measure, to try and get people working with different people, so that they can value and respect everybody for their qualities even if they are qualities which, by and large, are not seen to be acceptable.

Answering back

Each of the chapters in Part 2 has a section called 'Answering back'. I invited seven people to 'answer back' with responses to chapters. The intention is to have more than one perspective on each of the issues in Part 2 and to keep the thinking about them in process rather than concluded. Some of the contributors have addressed their response to me directly, using the second person 'you'. Others have made a more general response using the third person.

Deborah Chetcuti. On not staying stuck in a zero-sum game

My ideas about self-esteem started off with thinking about self-esteem and achievement. My initial ideas were very similar to the current orthodoxy regarding self-esteem. Firstly, I thought that self-esteem was something personal and individual and did not have anything to do with others. Secondly, I thought that there was a direct relationship between self-esteem and achievement; that is, that high achievement resulted in high self-esteem and vice versa that low achievement resulted in low self-esteem. Thirdly, I was under the impression that more of anything, more marks, more beauty, more money meant more self-esteem.

My ideas started to change when I started to work with students in schools and when I started to carry out research in the area of assessment. I started to realize through my conversations with students, with colleagues and most of all through self-reflection that, firstly, self-esteem was always a response to relationships with others, with parents, family members, friends and teachers; secondly, that achievement and self-esteem could not be treated as linear independent variables but that other factors such as gender, class, social positioning also had an important role to play; thirdly, that having more of things did not necessarily mean having more self-esteem.

Perhaps I can explain further, how I have come to these ideas. I would like to share with you the stories of two girls, myself and one of my students, a generation of about 15 years between us but educated in the same girls' private school, with the same drive for success and both with parents demanding this success. What struck me when I was talking to Maria was the similarity of our experiences yet the very different outcome. I was talking to a class of students about self-esteem and the development of an identity and I shared with them my experience of how I always felt that I was valued by my parents for my success in examinations, how my parents always questioned why I came second and not first, how I was asked why it was 99 and not 100 and how only a first all around seemed to please them. I talked to the students about how I always managed to achieve but despite my achievement, my self-esteem was not very high and I always devalued myself. I tried to explain that I felt that the reason behind this was that I did not feel loved and valued for who I was as a person but only for what I was achieving. This is similar to what you have described in your introduction about Martin Luther King who talks about not being loved by your neighbour unless you could love yourself. I continued to talk to the students about my own experiences with other pupils who felt that they were only valued by the results which they obtained in their examinations and who felt that they were failures if they did not achieve the right results. I talked about the importance which the Maltese educational system placed on examinations and how one of the pupils who I had interviewed had described herself as 'not clever because the exam tells me so . . . I only get five or seven . . . I'll never go to university.' Another pupil told me: 'My whole life depended on the results of my exams . . . I did quite well and am very happy . . . but what if I had not done so well . . . would I have become a different person?'

At this point Maria spoke up and said that she had a similar experience but that she did not agree with me when I said why I had a low self-esteem. She then described her experience to me. She had attended the same private school (with in some cases the same teachers) that I had attended more than 10 years previously and she described how her parents treated her in the same way, how they asked her why she did not get a 100 instead of a 99, how they shouted at her when she did not do so well. But the difference for her was that she still felt good about herself. In her own words, she said that her parents always told her, 'You are achieving what you are achieving for yourself and not for us.' So she always tried to be the best or one of the best but for her own satisfaction and for nothing else. In her view, it was the school rather than her parents which made her compete and vie with her friends for the rewards given to students on each prize day.

So what is the difference between me and Maria, similar parents, similar schools and yet two very different individuals: myself always doubting myself and Maria appearing to be confident of herself. I tried to think about this and my first reaction was to think that perhaps Maria had not reflected deeply enough on the issues and had not yet realized how much she depended on examinations to value herself. I asked her how she thought that her life would be without exams and she said that her parents would then value her on the way in which she was doing her job – again placing value on performance – so perhaps there is not so much difference there. But another important difference between the two of us arises out of the description of ordinary differences and trying to fit into the groups. As you describe in your chapter, differences are ordinary and exist in every form of our lives – yet it is the way in which we interpret these differences which determines in my view the kind of identity we develop of ourselves. Maria explained this to me:

> What was important for me was that I always tried to be an all rounder . . . I tried to do other things other than being good academically . . . I played basketball and did dancing and that made me better accepted by my friends . . . I wasn't a nerd who studied all the time . . . I did other things as well.

This perhaps explains a bit of what you mean by ordinary differences and the differences they make. In my case, my difference made me accepted by my parents but not by my peers and that left me with a feeling of something missing. In the case of Maria, her differences became ordinary because having many talents she could fit in with different groups like a chameleon. She could be a good student and gain the praise of parents and teachers and she could be an ordinary student interested in sports and dancing and gain the admiration of her peers. This made her feel, in her own words, 'accepted by all and with a good self-esteem'.

Therefore, I agree with your attempt to try and understand difference because I feel that it is this difference which needs to be focused on. In my experience, as parents, as teachers and as students we try to categorize individuals and strive so much to be fair that we try to make everyone the same whereas we should be celebrating this difference. A small anecdote which happened to me and illustrates this clearly is the way in which my mother reasons. We were three girls and she tries very hard to be fair with all of us and show no preferences, yet at times she does this at the expense of our own individuality. Recently, we had a cousin's wedding. The wedding was in the morning and I showed up at the wedding wearing a hat. Her first reaction, was, 'Oh no! Your sisters are going to be upset because they aren't wearing a hat. You should have all agreed to wear or not wear a hat.'

Anyway where is all this getting me? I can only share my own experiences but I feel that this is typical of why sometimes problems are created. We strive to be similar to each other, to fit the stereotypes – and if we do not fit in then we feel that we are not respected and valued by others and that therefore we do not value ourselves.

This is also the case in our classrooms – we leave no space for diversity and from an early age we give up on creativity at the expense of similarity. This starts from as early as kindergarten where we try and make children all colour in the same way, using the same colours and so on – whereas they could come up with fantastic pictures even if a bit surrealistic. Then we want them to pass the 11 plus examination, because if they do not pass they will be different and labelled not clever – and we do this at the expense of other areas of learning and intelligences. Then they need to go to university and we create images of what our children should be like and should be doing at the expense of difference and in the name of belonging.

In my opinion, it is a question of trying to juggle who you really are as an individual through the web of your experiences and who you need to be in order to fit in and be accepted in certain groups. It is easy if you find a group and fit in with that particular group but in the case of someone like myself who tries to juggle being a mother with being an educator and an academic at the university, the task becomes almost impossible because within every group you are treated as different: you are not a good mother, because you have a career; you are not a good educator, because you do not devote 24 hours of your day to doing your work; and you are not a good academic, because again you do not spend 12 hours of your work behind a desk reading a book. So where does that leave me – really stuck in the zero-sum game . . .

But, as an educator, I really believe in doing something to help students develop the best identity which they can for themselves. And this can be done, as you have stated, by really developing ways in which differences can be taken for granted and where they can be celebrated instead of becoming a hindrance. In assessment, what we are trying to do in Maltese schools is to try and introduce the idea of 'portfolio assessment'. We have started this with our student teachers in order to help them grow professionally, as well as to provide them with a tool through which they can really show who they are as teachers and what they are capable of as professionals. In schools the idea is similar, in that we are trying to move away from the evaluation of pupils on the basis of a single grade obtained in an examination, towards a profile of their successes and achievements which can show their various talents and intelligences and also show the process of their learning rather than only the product. This is of course still very much at the initial stages and though the idea is accepted as an idea, there are still many practical issues which need to be dealt with.

Max Biddulph. Consistency, stoicism and liberal (not permissive) attitudes

In this brief response, I want to explore two things. My first reply will be to give some general reactions personally to some of the issues that the chapter raises. My second reply will be to consider the implications for practitioners, which I will do via a reflection on a live and ongoing piece of current classroom practice.

Personal responses

I suppose my first response to the chapter is one of relief. At last, someone has had the courage to interrogate and problematize what is meant by the term 'self-esteem'. I have to confess to having being particularly wedded to the term in the past and felt a degree of defensiveness when I read it being questioned in this chapter. I know that some of this is due to my own 'story'. In my own personal development, I have seen myself at different times as many things, each generating a new 'self-descriptor'. I am struck by the potency of simply making these statements; I am also aware of their contradictory nature and the complexity that they reveal; I resonate with the observations that are made about Hannah Arendt and her identities in this respect. I also have to confess to a degree of discomfort in referring to my self-descriptors, not just because they are revealing, particularly in group situations, but because I associate a degree of emotional pain and struggle with some of them.

Here is an argument which, for me, is quite central in the chapter and relates strongly to my experience of life: that is that 'difference' is a key aspect of group experience. Layer on top of that the social, political and emotional culture of the environment and you have a heady cocktail of influences which can affect the self-esteem of individuals.

I have come to recognize my 'assertive voice'. Assertiveness as a communication style may have a certain significance for readers from Western cultures and less for those from elsewhere. Part of its appeal for me is that it is based not just on rights but also on responsibilities, which by definition require a more proactive stance on the part of individuals who are trying to communicate assertively. I want to share two pieces of personal learning here that relate to self-esteem. The first relates to an aspect of my behaviour, which I dislike the most – passivity. I intuitively associate it with low self-esteem – when I experience it, I know that the old introjects are reclaiming some ground. This raises questions about where and when we acquire introjects or disempowering messages that are internalized by individuals.

I was reminded of my second insight when I read the question which asks if high self-esteem is some sort of automatic entitlement. I know that I do not have universally high self-esteem on a 24/7 basis and I have learned not to expect it. My sense is that my opinion of myself has many compartments, some of which may be better off than others in the 'self-esteem stakes' at any given point in time. It is hard for me to pinpoint the source of this perception – I would say that it has evolved over time with experience. It feels the product of reality. I am reminded of the salutary words: 'Life is difficult' (Scott Peck 1987: 15).

Professional responses

Stepping back from my initial defensiveness relating to the dissection of the term 'self-esteem', I have to acknowledge a private unease that I have been harbouring for some time. In my work with professionals in the field of sex and relationships education (SRE), the term self-esteem is used extensively. I have frequently used it myself when working on scenarios in training, when I have suggested that we as workers need to 'boost the client's self-esteem'. Typically, the verbal response from participants to this suggestion is broadly supportive – non-verbally, however, the message I receive back communicates confusion and curiosity. My interpretation of this aspect is that it relates to exactly how, in practical terms, self-esteem can be raised. This is the point where I want to say that the deconstruction of the term in this chapter is incredibly helpful – the discussion brings clarity to the range of specific phenomena that are frequently subsumed under the term 'self-esteem'. In SRE, for example, if what we are really aiming for is increased motivation and confidence in using condoms, then it is really enabling for educators to be this specific.

Interestingly, SRE, in my experience, can often act as a key point of engagement for young people around issues of diversity, self-knowledge and, by implication, self-esteem. A case in point is a personal, social health education (PSHE) group of 12–13-year-olds that I have been teaching for two years now in a UK secondary school. In the time that we have been together I have the sense that I have been part of a process that has moved from group formation when they became a new class in the school in Year 7, to group conflict and more recently into conflict resolution. At the height of the group conflict stage, I observed zero-sum games being acted out on many occasions. Competition between group members was fierce, physical and verbal intimidation was a frequent occurrence and very few people felt heard, either literally or in the sense that Rogers defines in terms of 'emotional hearing' (Rogers 1983; Rogers and Feiburg 1994). Bullying was taking place inside and outside the lesson – a lot of tears were shed in this stage.

I include myself in the list of casualties – I felt stressed, very challenged by their behaviour and at times totally invisible. My own 'teacher self-esteem' took a bashing and I frequently had the experience of feeling deskilled and being ineffective. My tried and tested PSHE teaching and learning styles seemed to fail miserably. In our first circle time together a succession of individuals announced how badly life had treated them and then proceeded to put down other people. That led to my decision to abandon this activity for 12 months. This led to a much more rigid and structured regime in lessons, which worked to a point but did not provide an opportunity to work on what I would identify as key social skills that can take place in the circle.

It is difficult to be precise about the exact nature of the turning point – I think a number of developments coincided. In my role as teacher, I think that I have done two things that have contributed to our new situation. The first has been to forge a deeper relationship with class members via one-to-one interactions and inter-actions with small groups. I have tried to model authenticity and congruency in these interactions, especially when giving praise. The second intervention has been to extend our SRE work, which has been in direct response to needs that I have picked up from the group.

Group members have also resolved some of their disputes, and the maturation process is also impacting on their behaviour.

To my delight, we have resumed our work in the circle, where participants are gradually honing the skills of listening and speaking. Most significantly, a critical moment was reached in the group recently when individuals spoke with great matur-ity and sensitivity about sexual identity. What made the moment critical for me was the fact that an aspect of human diversity was discussed in such an accepting way, in marked contrast to some of the earlier behaviours expressed by group members.

The experience has filled me with great hope and I want to make some obser-vations about self-esteem here. The first concurs with the arguments in the chapter that self-esteem is complex. The second is that despite the best will in the world, self-esteem improvement does not take place overnight, it is a process. Teachers can make a difference in this respect by modelling consistency, stoicism, and values and attitudes that are truly liberal and not permissive. I think that a key to moving forward has to be in the relationship that develops between the teacher and the young people. Where I would extend the scope of the chapter is to highlight the significance of teacher self-esteem – friends and supporters in staff rooms are worth their weight in gold.

Notes

1 See also work in psychology on self-inclusive groups (for example, Hogg and Abrams 2001).

2 We use the term 'reactive' as being relatively neutral, theoretically. It is, however, related to Nietzsche's *ressentiment*, and to Foucault's 'resistance' and 'reverse discourse' (Nietzsche 1887; Foucault 1979, 1980).

3   There may be a statistical 'norm' in those cases where difference can reason-
    ably be assigned a numerical value – but that is a very different thing from 'the
    norm' as something to which someone should aspire.
4   See also Chapter 8.

6 Empowerment: something to shout about

Introduction

Expressing yourself, knowing that what you have to say has value, making your presence felt: this is to have a voice. But it is hard to say what you mean, and hard to get anything done about it: doing either is likely to annoy other people who have power. It is even harder to try to work with others so as to increase their powers of expression. To manage all this for oneself or for others is, so it is often claimed, empowerment. In this chapter, the value and danger of speaking for oneself – and trying to give everyone a fair say – will be discussed, especially in relation to the kind of power that it gives.

As two external examiners for a doctorate, Richard Winter and I had institutional power, and were required to exercise it. We were required to use our voice in the report to the university, but during that process the voice of Moira Laidlaw, the candidate, was confined to giving responses in the oral examination. We, the two examiners, discussed the dilemmas of examining practice-based research. We decided to use our discussion as the basis for an article that we subsequently published, carefully anonymizing the three specific cases we referred to in order (so we thought) not to abuse the voice and power we were exercising. Luckily, we consulted all three people whose cases we were to use, and while two slightly preferred to remain anonymous, Moira was quite clear that we should use her real name – which we did – precisely so that we should not abuse our voice and power. Moira wanted to be free to comment on the processes of her own examination, and has done so. In the course of this negotiation, I learnt something about ethics, voice and the distribution of power. And about the specificity of complex cases.

Moira subsequently published a later piece of research, in a wonderful article that traced her involvement with Sally, a black pupil in her class at a secondary school in Bath, a part of the country with few black people in it (Laidlaw 1999). In this case, Moira, as the schoolteacher, had institutional power and was required to exercise it. The paper gives an account of how she carefully considers the importance of listening, with love, to her pupils, and responding to them with fairness. The paper turns on an incident in which Sally, suddenly and uncharacteristically, bursts out in fury about the white curriculum of the school – perhaps feeling Moira's class is a safe enough place to voice these feelings. The paper shows how Moira learns more about making room for other voices, about how to give them power, about greater sensitivity as an educator. She explores how she helps Sally to 'move from a position of resentment and anger to one in which she is making judgements and decisions which have the power to direct her life for herself' (Laidlaw 1999). Sally, like Moira before her, chose to be named, and she participated with Moira in negotiating how the evidence in the article is presented.

The structures in which we all (me, Richard, Moira, Sally) spoke and acted are relatively unchanged. The authority systems of PhD examining and school teaching remain as they were. But there have been small changes. The explicit airing of dilemmas makes some difference to the sense of self and self-respect of those who are the object of them, as well as of those who experienced them. So there are some changes in how they act. Moreover, an article can have some impact on those who read it as well as on those who write it. Some few things are changing in relation to the examining of practice-based doctorates. Some things have changed in the education of the girls in Moira's school. And the ripples from all of these events may have spread outwards in ways that would be impossible to track (Dadds 1995).

The story I have just told is a 'little story', with all the limitations and strengths of such stories. It is in my voice, but it includes the echoes of other little stories told by other people. Since it is specific, it does not reduce all the characters to ciphers. It is not a generalized account about 'the PhD candidate' or 'the examiner', nor 'the black schoolgirl' and her 'white teacher'. Instead, it refers to particular people in specific contexts. If it had been told by any of the other participants (or witnesses) it would have been expressed differently, and had different consequences. It is told with the intention of having an effect on what educators do about making space for diverse voices.

Little stories and questions of voice and empowerment

The term 'little stories' is useful in this chapter because it links voice to narrative by taking the particular perspective of an individual seriously: that is, the individual as situated in particular circumstances in all their complexity. At the same time, it is a term that carries the implication of a link to grander concerns like education, social justice and power. The term 'little stories' is a resonant one perhaps because it is ambiguous. Some of the reasons for using the term are given in Chapter 3.

The ambiguities in the term 'little stories' are productive as long as there is enough common meaning to allow useful communication. The idea underpins a loosely coherent set of approaches to social justice in which they are seen as a way of representing diversity, in which people are authorities of their own experience, and which readily include the emotional as well as the rational aspects of social justice. Stories can be told visually, and also in poems, imagery, movement (dance) and so on.[1]

Examples of little stories show these characteristics, at the same time as demonstrating the range of different ways of producing and using them. Consider the following examples:

1   Marion Dadds's beautifully evoked, research-based account of one teacher's action research and the effects on her, her colleagues and the teaching in her school is a story linked to general themes of action research, its impact and its effect on the self (Dadds 1995).

2   Richard Winter has developed a method for professionals to guide their own learning through the creative use of both fiction and fact in writing collections of stories: 'patchwork texts' (Winter *et al.* 1999).

3   Max Biddulph sensitively uses a series of his interviews with gay/bisexual educators so that they can tell their stories, but anonymously and without outing themselves (Biddulph 1997, 2003).

4   Ghazala Bhatti weaves the life stories of her Asian pupils and of her continuing education students so as to engage the reader's imagination about the effects of race, class and gender on personal engagements with education systems (Bhatti 1999, 2001).

5   Phil Mignot has given (mostly Asian) young men a way of telling their little stories of their career aspirations by encouraging them to take photographs and then use them to create montages (Mignot 2000a, b).

6   I use a series of informal conversations with a group of educators to highlight our own different little stories in relation to our common concern for social justice in education (Griffiths 2002).

There are dangers. Little stories are told by individual human beings. On the other hand, as the examples in the previous paragraph show, they are stories of individuals as belonging to groups (teachers, learners, young people) or to classes of people (by sexuality, race, gender, social class and so on). So there is a danger that little stories can be merged into stereotypes. Or they may be merely anecdotal, uncritical and self-validating. Telling one's story may help in self-realization but may also be an exercise in self-delusion. Voice has to be treated with the same criticality as other autobiographical expressions – what I have called 'critical autobiography' (Griffiths 1995) – linking individual perspectives with the broader picture. But there is good reason to risk these dangers. Little stories can show the limitations and inaccuracies of the broader picture. They can also be combined into bigger pictures, but not in such a way as to blur the edges into generalizations.

But why should little stories be of significance at all? They may be a way to enhance self-confidence but they may also feed vanity. They may link selves to wider concerns, but so what? Perhaps the exchange of stories is no more than pleasant conversation: absorbing for the participants but of no wider interest. Something of the sort is suggested in the following bleak stanza (Lear 'The theologian's tale', *Tales of a Wayside Inn*):

> Ships that pass in the night, and speak each other in passing;
> Only a signal shown and a distant voice in the darkness;
> So on the ocean of life we pass and speak one another.
> Only a look and a voice; then darkness again and a silence.

Lear's vision may describe some kinds of speaking. But voice can signify something more. Another poet writing in bleak circumstances – his blindness coinciding with the Restoration and the loss of his cherished commonwealth – asserts the value of voice[2] (Milton *Paradise Lost*, VII 24–8):

> More safe I sing with mortal voice, unchanged
> To hoarse or mute, though fall'n on evil days,
> On evil days though fall'n, and evil tongues;
> In darkness, and with dangers compassed round,
> And solitude;

Milton, unlike Lear, is referring to a voice that speaks to some purpose. How the purpose might be achieved is alluded to as follows (*Paradise Lost*, VII 30–1):

> Still govern thou my song,
> Urania, and fit audience find, though few.

Milton asserts the need for an audience, fit audience, other than the muse, Urania.

A voice always speaks in context, and, inevitably, part of the context is the audience. Caution is in order: an audience may have no intention of listening, or it may listen in order to control and silence. But 'fit audience' can be found: a listener who is simply trying to understand; or someone who recognizes a similar voice and engages with the speaker by challenging, probing, arguing and perhaps expanding on the original expression. And when a fit audience is found, it may be that a difference can be made. The voice may have an effect, may have power, may be empowered. But there have been strong claims made that the use of the terms voice and empowerment is a kind of confidence trick, promising more than can be delivered.

Is empowerment all self-delusion and/or a confidence trick? A number of critics have urged the argument that 'empowerment' is indeed either one or the other or both. Jennifer Gore's arguments have been particularly significant and influential (Gore 1993, 1997). She points out the meaning of em-power-ment as something that is given away by someone who has power to someone who has not. Focusing on feminist and critical pedagogy, she argues that this shows that researchers appear to be working with 'a notion of power as property' that is 'repressive but reclaimable for productive and democratic purposes'. But in that case, she argues, feminist and critical pedagogies and action research methods have failed to be transformative and emancipatory because they have very little influence over the whole context. They cannot empower, even though that is what they promise. In similar vein, Michael Fielding (1996) argues that the term 'empowerment' is an example of language closing down rather than opening up possibilities. He cautions that: 'We face the emergence of notions like empowerment which marginalize or erase the very promise they seem to offer' (Fielding 1996: 31).

Gore's argument is powerful and important, but it has limited range. There is more than one way of understanding 'power' (see discussion in Griffiths 1998a). Similarly for empowerment. It may mean power that is given away, but it may also mean power that is taken for oneself.[3] There is no reason to suppose that such power is a kind of property, or that having it is an all or nothing affair. There can be empowerment short of the transformation of the structures of education. There is room for more than one interpretation of empowerment, connected, but different in scope and intention, and dependent on context. Claims for empowerment range from gaining a sense of self as agent, through coming to understand one's class, race, gender and other positionings, to mov-ing the immediate context forward, and, occasionally, to large-scale policy and revolution. Claims to research leading to people 'being empowered' or even just 'feeling empowered' include those based on an individual (or a small group of individuals) coming to act expressively and on principle. Consider the case of Sally. Think of Maxine's, Syble's and Anne's stories in Chapter 2. All of them gained power through an understanding of their positioning. Gore herself has not given up on feminist and critical pedagogies. Fielding still uses the term 'empowerment' despite his stated reservations (Fielding 2002).

Even if empowerment is possible, is not a confidence trick, many claims of getting or giving a voice are betrayals or, at best, self-delusion. There are serious criticisms that giving a voice is just a kind of ventriloquism; or that hearing the voice of relatively powerless people gives relatively more powerful ones a management tool with which to control them.

A kind of ventriloquism occurs when managers, teachers, policy makers and researchers express their own views but use the words of less powerful people to give the argument a spin of consultation. In an influential article, Kum-Kum Bhavani drew a distinction between 'empowerment' and 'giving a voice' (Bhavani 1988). She pointed out how 'giving a voice' by using, for instance, direct speech extracts in a piece of ethnographic research may confer an appearance of authenticity that is disempowering rather than empowering. She points out cases in which 'giving a voice' masks the reproduction of damaging stereotypes. However, as Iram Siraj-Blatchford (1994: 25) notes, it is important not to confuse arguments against merely quoting the direct speech of research respondents with research strategies in which respondents are 'given the opportunity to "talk back"'. Using the example of race, she affirms that, for black people, finding a voice can come of being 'given their colour'. She writes: 'What is important is finding a "voice" that engages in critical reflection, in resistance to domination, and in affirmation of the liberation struggle.'

In a useful article discussing how voice is being used to try to increase 'social inclusion' for young people, Hadfield and Haw (2001) detail different ways in which that voice can be articulated. They point out, however, that the contexts in which such voices are heard and whom they are heard by may be used as a subtle form of silencing. Fielding makes a similar case for young people in schools, arguing that, while student voice in schools may be 'genuinely new, exciting and emancipatory', it may also be the 'entrenchment of existing assumptions and intentions using student or pupil voice as an additional mechanism of control' (Fielding 2001). There are echoes here of Edward Said's ground-breaking study of 'orientalism', in which he showed how successive governments have managed colonized peoples by listening to their voices in order to rule them more effectively (Said 1978). But the existence of danger does not imply abandoning the task, only being aware of the risks. All these authors are enthusiastic advocates of listening to voices. Their cautions and warnings are intended to increase the chance that voices will be used for democratic renewal, for emancipation, to increase the chances of social inclusion.

Empowerment through voice

We all have our little stories to tell, and, if we value ourselves and others enough, we know that it is worth telling them. Each little story gains significance from its links with grand aspirations. In bell hooks's words:

> Moving from silence into speech is for the oppressed, the colonized, the exploited, and those who stand and struggle side by side a gesture of defiance that heals, that makes life and new growth possible. It is that act of speech of 'talking back,' that is no mere gesture of empty words, that is the expression of our movement from object to subject – the liberated voice.
>
> (hooks 1989: 9)

Good story telling is an art, dependent on the teller, the listener and the context, as well as on the story itself. The cautions sounded in the previous section have pointed to the importance of getting all of these right: especially finding listeners who are not intending to exploit or silence the story, and ensuring that the teller is not merely ventriloquizing. However, even in imperfect conditions, stories and story telling can be powerful in a number of ways. Some of these are: self-expression, validation, solidarity, increasing the air space and interrupting.

Self-expression: finding a listener

As Milton says, telling a story requires the teller to 'fit audience find, though few'. The listener has something to learn from this encounter, of course, as I remark below, but the activity also benefits the speaker. Having a listener helps the story teller to find the words, get them into order and craft a story. All of this helps the speaker to reflect on herself as the agent in the story. It is her little story, after all. This has an impact on how she approaches the rest of her life, in the light of what came before. So she is empowered to act in the light of that.

During a series of informal conversations with a group of educators I was given a strong reminder of the impact that having a listener can make on the speaker. Three years after taking part in the 'Fairness project' (Griffiths 1998a), members of the group remembered the interview in the first phase of that project in which they had been asked, individually, to reflect on their own experiences. This, they told me, had been significant to them. I had not expected this. I had thought of this interview only as a kind of ground-clearing. And I would have thought that all of these people have professional roles (headteachers, deputy heads, advisers and university lecturers) that give them plenty of opportunities to express their points of view. This is the kind of thing they said:

> It gave me an opportunity to talk about things that often you never really talk about. Only in certain situations do you feel you can explore those kinds of issues. I suppose that gave me the opportunity to think about those. It's not part of your everyday job. Even in teaching. (Jacky)

> What I remember about it is – well, it seemed to me like it had several component parts. I remember our one-to-one conversation, and I remember my reaction to receiving the transcript . . . As I think I said at the time, I was surprised that I sounded vaguely coherent and articulate. I guess a lot of the ums and ahs have been deleted. But even so. (Max)

[One of the main] things I remember . . . where discussions were supporting me in tracking where I'd come from, and perhaps why particular issues were important to me. I think that made quite an impact
in terms of recognizing that, perhaps a bit more explicitly. (Nada)

These energetic, competent people are articulating just how important it is in
terms of their own agency and direction to have a listener for their 'little
stories' of working for social justice in education.

Validation: finding similar voices

The patchwork texts that Richard Winter asks his students to create depend on
their finding similar voices among their fellow professionals. He describes the
method. The course participants form small working groups (four or five people).
Each person produces short pieces of writing – stories – reflecting on aspects
of their professional practice. The stories are shared (Winter *et al.* 1999: 10):

To begin with, interpretations of the meaning of the piece are
exchanged by the readers; but then further questions are raised . . .
The group sharing process suggests to the participants how they
might continue their writing and their reflections.

This process depends on each member of the group recognizing the others as
similar, not the same. Their voices are similar enough to the original for it to be
helpfully challenged by the listeners. The process is one that validates the
original voice. The challengers do not shout down or silence it, but help it
expand and get richer.

Michele Foster brings out a different source of empowerment from finding
similar voices: the preservation of memories for the benefit of future collective
action by setting the record straight for those who come afterwards (Foster
1993). She was struck by the lack of academic literature about black American
teachers, and, worse, that what there was tended to be negative portrayals
written by outsiders. She writes:

There were many times when I interacted with my subjects that I
heard my own voice in theirs, voices that had waged a continuing
struggle against an analysis of their lives imposed by outsiders . . .
seeking to reorder their realities to conform to an external agenda.
(Foster 1994: 145)

She was creating an archive by producing an account told by these voices
similar but not identical to her own, and all of them different from those of
the mainstream. She was contributing to an alternative source of historical

documentation for use by anyone who needed to find validation of their own voice in the echoes of earlier ones.

Solidarity: speaking together with others

Marion Dadds wrote her book about one teacher's action research as an act of solidarity (Dadds 1995). At least I, for one, read it like that. She writes about the particularities of Vicki, an ex-student from her INSET (in-service education for teachers) course, and the fate of her three pieces of action research carried out as course work. At the same time, the book is an account of her own action research about the INSET course. Dadds works hard to make sure the reader knows that Vicki is not meant to be 'typical'. The detail about her specific situation and particular character ensure that. Nor is Marion Dadds typical of INSET tutors, in her approach, her way of presenting the material or the conclusions she draws. But for all that, the book sounds a strong, clear argument for action research, for INSET grounded in teacher action research and for the ways in which all such passionate research can benefit the person doing it, their students (both children and adults) and their colleagues.

This is a book rooted in the traditions of action research and its literature. It is meant to be read by, among others, those of us who write articles and books drawing on action research (for instance, in this chapter, Moira Laidlaw and Richard Winter). The book speaks together with all us others in solidarity. Solidarity is not unison. Marion's own voice remains as distinct as mine, Moira's or Richard's. But we speak together, in the sense of conversation, as a group, and taking up much more air space than any one of us could on our own.

Increasing the air space: listening to unfamiliar voices

Mention has been made of the value of listening. The attentive listener has much to learn. What has been said about validation and solidarity shows how much there is to learn from discovering similar voices. However, there is also much to learn from listening to little stories told by unfamiliar voices.

Little stories trouble and disturb the taken-for-granted simplifications with which we understand those parts of the world of which we know little. The voices heard in little stories are inherently, intractably, grittily human: therefore, they are unsimplified and difficult to fit into previous simplified rationales. Consider the stories made available by Ghazala Bhatti, Phil Mignot and Max Biddulph. They will be unfamiliar to those readers who are not marginalized in the same way as the tellers of the stories. Ghazala Bhatti recounts the stories of continuing education students, recognizably of working class, and/or racially excluded groups, and of both sexes. However, they both do and do not fit the usual stereotypes, and are eloquent about the effects of their encounters with education (Bhatti 2001). The young Asian men whom Phil Mignot works with are rarely given a chance to express their career aspirations in relation to their hopes about their lives. Finally, homophobia ensures that gay and bisexual educators often feel the need to stay in the closet in order to continue to teach. So people outside this group, and many within it, hardly ever encounter the kinds of little stories that Max Biddulph makes available. If we can be attentive, a fit audience, the authors of these little stories have a lot to teach all of us, if only because such authors do not usually have access to the air space.

Interrupting: speaking up

When I was in the kindergarten, we used to enjoy chanting a rhyme that went like this:

> (Softly) We are the quiet boys,
> (More softly) We are the quiet boys,
> (Very softly) We are the quiet boys,
> (Whispering) But sometimes . . .
> (Shouting) *We make a big, big noise.*

Perhaps we were learning a useful lesson. For those who are habitually quiet, it is important that ways are found to be loud sometimes. In the incident mentioned earlier, Sally was right to explode, especially since it was uncharacteristic of her. Sometimes the rest of the world needs to be made to listen. Doing so breaks the rules, of course. That is what was such fun about our kindergarten rhyme! But the rules need to be broken when they underpin such widespread silencing of so many. A tiny proportion of people have the megaphone most of the time, and, worse, come to believe that they are the only ones who say anything worth hearing. As a teacher researcher commented about her own research related to inclusion (England and Brown 2001: 369): '[Teacher] research also needs to become an on-going disruption of our immersion in the discourses, which serve to maintain the status quo of supposed social roles within this world.' The next section includes ideas about ways of doing this difficult thing.

Getting real: listen to this!

Each chapter in Part 2 has a section called 'Getting real'. The purpose is to move from an examination of ideas in general terms – where examples are used to illuminate the theorizing – to a more practical perspective. It is also important to see what practical use can be made of the ideas in specific circumstances: for *real individuals*, with their *specific socio-political positions* (race, class, gender, sexuality and so on), in *particular educational contexts* (classrooms, schools, tertiary institutions) and *in relation to identifiable communities* (their own members, local communities, advisers, universities, national or international networks of educators). This section is not intended to give lots of tips for lessons or policies. Instead, it is intended to inspire and illuminate, by showing the ideas in action, in all their contextual specificity, enacted by real people. It is hoped that these examples will help educators to rethink what they, themselves, might do in their own contexts.

Pupils talk back to the press

Tony Cotton is an education lecturer. He has a strong commitment to improving social justice, whether teaching, researching or doing consultancy work. In this account he describes working, in partnership with a local teacher, for action around 'empowerment and voice' for young people (and their teachers) in a secondary school in the city centre. These young people are of various ethnic backgrounds, and of both sexes. They live in some of the poorest areas of the city. They are unlikely to be from middle-class backgrounds. Tony describes what happened when Ofsted reported on their school.

I arrive at the school this week realizing that today may be different from other days. I have been working with a group of 15- and 16-year-old pupils at the school every week during their GCSE drama sessions. The question we are working on is, 'What is it like to be here?' We have been working very hard at coming to an articulation of this for the last two terms.

But today is the day after the Ofsted report on the school was released to the press. The headline in the local paper screamed 'Another City School Slammed', and went on to describe in detail the school's perceived failings. I had already been in conversation with the journalist who wrote the piece, one of those 'do you know who I am conversations' when we attach some importance to our doctorate and imagine it may give us power to do something on behalf on someone else.

As with most of these conversations I was left feeling as though I had no power at all.

I met the teacher and we decided we would have to ditch the plan altogether to allow the young people we were working with to express how they felt. We had no option as we wished to remain faithful to the project's aims. The whole project so far had taken 'voice' as a starting point, but with a view that finding and articulating a 'voice' is immensely problematic. We don't just know how we feel about our situation – we must work very hard to find ways of describing our situation that sum up for us 'what it is like to be here'. The aim of such a project is to work together with young people within schools so that they become analytical of the system of schooling they are embroiled in rather than judgemental. That they develop a sense of how schooling positions us, as well as how we position ourselves. After several weeks engaged in telling, evaluating, analysing and researching individual stories about school, the group had concluded that the key issue for them was respect. How is respect played out in school, in all the relationships, student–teacher, student–student, student–family, and all the other relationships that impact on the everyday stuff of schooling?

So the students entered the drama space and sat in the circle. Silence at first. 'Have you seen the newspaper?' Some anger.

'Who does he think he is to write stuff like that?'

'How does he know what it's like here? He's never even visited the school.'

And so on. I ask the question, 'What would you like to do about it?' The clear reply, 'We want to get him in here and make him feel as bad as he has made us feel.'

My colleague has an idea. She suggests that we role-play this situation. I leave the room to re-enter as the journalist. When I come back into the space, the room is dark except for a spotlight on the chair in which I am to sit. I sit down and introduce myself, 'Hello, my name is Roy Warren, I'm a journalist on the *Post*. I heard that you wanted to ask me some questions.'

Then silence again, a tense, nervous silence. Then one of the girls turns to the teacher and says, 'It's no good, miss, we don't know what to say.' This group of very articulate, angry, perceptive, young people had completely lost any 'voice' they had.

We moved on – we agreed that neutral territory might be the best place for a meeting. The students worked at the exact questions they would want to ask, and how they could link these questions to the theme of 'respect'. They selected those who would represent the group and some weeks later the journalist agreed to meet four of the students at the university in which I worked. He also agreed to be videoed. I'll end this story with an extract from the interview – less of an interview perhaps and more of a chance for these young people to tell someone who had made them feel disempowered what it was like. This extract is 10 minutes into the conversation.

'Can we tell you how we felt when we read your article?'

'Yeah.'

'It makes you feel ashamed. Because that is the school that you go to. You're learning from teachers who have got bad reports and you're learning with children who've got bad reports. You think, "Am I one of those children who aren't doing very well?" It doesn't make you feel very good about yourself. Did you think about how we would feel when we read this stuff? You could have written it another way.'

'Yeah – but I had to be accurate. I just reported what Ofsted had said. If I had written a positive story and the top line had said that the school was failing it wouldn't have made any sense.'

'But you could have gone about it any way you liked. You're a reporter. You wouldn't like it if your daughter read this stuff about her school. You wouldn't like it if she was ashamed to go to school, if she hated going to school, if she felt bad about herself, not because of her school but because of what you had written.'

'No, I probably wouldn't. But what is it you think we should have done differently? How should I have written it?'

'I don't know. You can't ask me that. I'm not a reporter.'

From seeking invisibility to making contact with the outside world

Adrian finds that the young people in his classes can be helped by his PSE lessons on sex, sexuality and masculinity, even if they have to hide that fact in front of their peers, by joining in with the general macho culture. In order to do this he needed to 'make contact' and find his voice as source of his own empowerment.

I think the issue is more complex than just about sexuality. It's about masculinity also. The issue is a school, as I see it, in which the clientele present a slice of life. I'm talking about the pupils. They are as racist, sexist, homophobic, ablist, as they come. There are some wonderful staff who have been extraordinarily supportive to me. And there are some staff who are a slice of life.

For a long time I functioned as an individual who had this knowledge about himself. As far as I was concerned I was the only person who knew this thing about myself. That is a very lonely and isolated place to be. Can you imagine what it is like to be edited out? It's extraordinarily painful. I think lesbian and gay people have to deal with the difficulty of invisibility. So now I have made contact with the outside world on this issue it is like a dynamo.

I'm quite interested in how I am now with young people. Let's start with the young people whom I teach sex education. I think I'm far less hurt by homophobia. I still get pointed out when walking between buildings:

'There's the queer!'

'There's the pouff!'

'We all know about him.'

That kind of stuff. I think I'm less defensive without self-disclosing in lessons. So if they say, which they do virtually every week, 'So are you gay, then?' 'Well, what if I was? Would that matter then?' I say. The bright people there will notice I've not said 'No,' and I haven't outed myself. And I don't take any crap. Like at the end of a lesson, some months ago they shouted from three storeys down, 'Fucking queer!'

So what I always do is make an intervention. So I got my mates in high places, the following Monday morning gently to take this class to one side and say, 'Look, we don't know who said this, but you need to know this is totally unacceptable, etcetera, etcetera.'

Answering back

Each of the chapters in Part 2 has a section called 'Answering back'. I invited seven people to 'answer back' with responses to chapters. The intention is to have more than one perspective on the issues in Part 2 and to keep the thinking about them in process rather than concluded. Some of the contributors have addressed their response to me directly, using the second person 'you'. Others have made a more general response using the third person.

Ghazala Bhatti. So, are you, the reader, empowered?

(A reply to Morwenna, and in memory of Mike's idiosyncrasies.)

In order successfully to extend an 'invitation for a dialogue' to more than one author, and, in response, to be able truly to listen to many replying voices expressed in different tones that fill many spaces (for there may be more than one air space!), it is crucial to write in an accessible manner. I liked the accessibility and conversational style of the text. Both the form and the content demonstrate the challenge of expressing complex ideas simply, especially as the issue of empowerment is imbued with abstractions. The text has to achieve at least two things simultaneously. It has to explore the notion of empowerment *per se*, while at the same time seeking to empower the participant/reader to some extent. If it does not do the latter, then the mutually constructed potential of 'empowerment' is somehow depleted, and real power remains confined within the first author's voice alone. The danger is that 'empowerment' can so easily become a rhetorical device, a mere play on words. It is a tall order. So, does the above chapter avoid the danger and achieve all this?

In her chapter, Griffiths reminds us of the ways in which other writers talk of empowerment. Gore (1993, 1997) and Fielding (1996), however, mean different things by empowerment. Their criticism of its effectiveness hinges on their particular expectations from empowerment's ability to deliver. But to deliver what? It is more a question of sharing the space on centre stage than 'gifting' or bestowing power. The giver may think she grows greater in the process of giving, but it is only the sharer who can truly 'empower'. Therein lies the paradox. It is only when 'the empowered' themselves recognize (in their own good time) that they have been empowered individually or collectively, emotionally and rationally, that empowerment can be said to have occurred. Self-delusion on the part of the one factitiously seeking to empower others poses a real danger, I agree. Moreover, in my experience at least, disempowered people do not always feel they are being empowered at the time when one might assume they are being 'empowered'. Some resist it, because in educational and social justice terms they have not ever before been given respect, or the responsibility for their own learning. Sometimes,

a long time after the event, and on reflection, comes the recognition of empowerment, almost like a delayed reaction, as a sort of flashback. Sally's unchecked
outburst in Moira's article is an affirmation and a recognition. Such is the complexity inherent in the notion of real empowerment. Empowerment is multidimensional and multilayered. It is multidimensional because there are as many types and
facets of empowerments as there are individuals. Besides, the understanding of
'empowerment' itself may differ over time. Its meaning does not remain static. It is
multilayered because it is only by peeling off false (self-protective?) layers that a
tiny part of the core is revealed. What empowers me today – an honest exchange of
ideas that are listened to, a single act of kindness, a little generosity of spirit – may
not have empowered me on a previous day. The cyclical spiral of learning based on
lived experience feeds on itself and grows in both directions, into the past and back
to the present.

It is mostly from the privileged position of relative power that we can begin to
talk of empowerment. Those who are not empowered sometimes do not talk of
empowerment to 'others' who are not like them, because they have suffered loss of
voice and power so often and so regularly that they believe it to be an illusion. An
example might help to explain what I mean. Three years ago I worked with a
27-year-old undergraduate student, Mike, to put together a research-based dissertation on single homeless people in London. During the process of writing he
struggled with his self-perceived academic difficulties. He battled against the
demands of the required precision in descriptive and analytical language. He felt
trapped by cold print. The reductive effect of 'black and white text' made him
doubt he would ever be able to convey even a small fraction of what he intended.
Try as hard as I might, for months I failed to persuade him that the process of
translating real encounters with raw experiences of life into mere words is inherently difficult, that it must make even skilled writers dither. Mike had been out of
formal education for over eight years. What had catapulted him back into facing his
inner fears was a desire to make a plea on behalf of those to whom he had dedicated
over eight years of his working life – single homeless men. Mike had a great rever-
ence for the printed word. He felt that somehow 'writing it all down' would leave a
record and transfer the responsibility for alleviating 'homelessness in such a rich
country' to policy makers and others with power. He spoke quietly, yet angrily and
powerfully, of the way you can tell if someone has slept rough on a cold night.

'It is the blue colour of their fingernails, Ghazala, and the state of their feet and
their shoes. Swollen feet don't fit normal shoes.'

It was humbling to watch Mike struggle with written words. His unembel-
lished spoken text, most aggressive when least loud, was powerful in its authenticity. But could he write effectively, or write at all? He fought back. He had huge
arguments with me about 'empowerment', though we didn't always call it that.
How could tutors in universities pretend to 'help' their students? Could I, as a South
Asian middle-class woman, probably living in some leafy suburb somewhere, working in the ivory tower, know the first thing about real homelessness? What would I

know about the deprivations of poverty-stricken, white, working-class male culture? *Educating Rita* was 'silly fiction'. Real life was something else. What was the point in obtaining a stupid degree anyway? He would go away and never ever come back. Never mind if one year's income had been wasted on travelling from London to Reading, getting drunk, buying books, getting into debt. Years of rage, of having been let down, of frustration with bad schooling experiences punctuated his sensitive outlook. Was I being ruthless, too demanding, in expecting him to write as well as other 'normal' undergraduates, I wondered? I could not let him get away without trying his personal best, even though we both knew how much he hated 'critical analysis'. That only led to more fear and rage. I stopped talking of 'empowerment' as he disappeared for days on end among the homeless and I worried about him.

It was a relief when the dissertation arrived on time for external examiners. It was a bigger surprise when the letter shown in Figure 6.1 arrived at my home address some days after the degree ceremony, in an untidy crumpled envelope,

LonDon
15/7/99.

Dear GHAZALA,

An overdue thank you for everything over the last academic year. I looked out for you at the ceremony but I left with my Mum before we found you.
I've been told my mum felt proud, so thanks for your help in giving her a good day.
I'm still hoping to study more and concentrate on some research – the part I really enjoyed – however, I also want to earn some money and have a holiday, so I'm looking at september 2000. I'd like to get in touch again to talk about further studying and, now its all over, to get some feedback on my last year.
I hope you enjoy your summer and your book gets noticed.

with love

Mike.

Figure 6.1 A letter from Mike

unstamped and written on a sheet torn from a notepad with droplets of rain smudging the thin blue lines.

Had I empowered Mike? Of course not. How could I? He has empowered me to continue to struggle to understand more people like him – pretty tough, even aggressive, on the outside and so vulnerable within. I do not remember discussing my book with him. Mike does know, however, that I would write about him one day and he said I could if I wished. It would be good if he got in touch and returned to research, which no doubt he will when he is ready.

Griffiths's chapter has worked in mysterious ways. It has reminded me of Mike, whom I had half-forgotten. It has persuaded me to share this little story. To return again to the question I raised at the beginning: 'Has the chapter succeeded in raising critically important issues about empowerment, and by implication about "real" education and about social justice?' Only the reader can answer that.

Notes

1 The relationship of research using oral history, narratives and so on to social activism is explored in LeCompte (1993). See also Greene (1995).

2 Plainly, Milton is not telling a 'little story'. However, it is widely held that this particular quotation refers to his own danger of imprisonment immediately after the Restoration.

3 From the *Compact Oxford English Dictionary* (1971): Empower: (1) (trans.) to invest legally or formally with power or authority; to authorise, license. (2) (trans.) to impart or bestow power to an end or for a purpose; to enable, permit. (3) (refl.) to gain or assume power over.

7 Partnership: consultation and conversation

Introduction

Partnership is at the heart of how my colleagues and I understand how we work in the Faculty of Education at Nottingham Trent University. This is how one of my colleagues puts it:

> There is a genuine desire in the Faculty to continue with partnership-based research which makes a difference to teachers' and kids' lives in school and to be rigorous and thoughtful and principled about it. If we can maintain this commitment, then we will be all right.

Another colleague explains why she has this commitment:

> I was working with children at my partnership project school last week alongside enthusiastic teachers, being observed by one of our students and being asked questions by interested parents. The outcomes of the work will be going to India with a teacher from the school to communicate information about the children's lives to children there. The data I have now collected as part of this project will I hope contribute through dissemination to a better understanding of the value of school linking in terms of geography, values learning and global citizenship. However, the process so far has been significant in already having an impact on the real lives of teachers and children and on their perceptions and understanding.

As educators, we would enjoy working in partnership, wouldn't we? For it is hardly surprising that anyone who chooses to teach might like partnership. To choose to teach is to choose to work with other people. Further, since everyone goes to school, we expect to meet a variety of people at work. A large part of the core job is to persuade everyone – students, colleagues at all levels and parents – to cooperate. But while we enjoy making successful partnerships work, we know, only too well, that they can be both wonderful and difficult – and often both at the same time.

My own professional experience of partnerships is indeed that they are both wonderful and difficult. I find that times when I have worked collaboratively in teaching and in research have been some of the most rewarding and energizing episodes of my working life. They have also included some of the most frustrating and destructive ethical minefields that I have ever encountered. Sometimes the same project can produce both. In general, I believe that some of the best, most productive, longest lived and most useful educational developments come about through partnership, so it is worth learning how to do them well.

Getting into partnership: getting into what exactly?

Partnership is claimed to be central to many institutions. Like so many other terms that have become clichés in education, 'partnership' is part of the rhetoric, part of every mission statement. There is a lot pushing teachers and other educators at all levels into partnership. For example, consider likely reasons for joining in with the following initiatives (covering each educational age phase): Sure Start, Best Practice Research Scholarships and university regional mergers. An ever-growing pile of policy initiatives related to education means that teaching, research and research-based development in institutions like schools, universities, support services and local government are being required to make closer links with a wide range of other groups.

The policy makers find themselves pushing at open doors. Partnership is not just a word in the mission statements or lists of aims and objectives, nor yet just in the funding applications. As a way of working, as a general approach, it is genuinely welcomed on all sides and often enthusiastically mentioned by teachers, headteachers, local authority staff, community representatives, teacher educators and governors. As with me and my colleagues quoted above, there is a widespread recognition that partnerships can be productive, energizing and powerful. So it is disappointing that some of these apparently open doors get stuck. The recommendations and policies of those involved in education, especially policy makers and decision makers at every level, often give the impression that partnerships can be set up and made to work easily, perhaps following a few simple guidelines. But the truth is that partnerships do not always work well. What is more, the time and resources needed to nurture them is in increasingly short supply, due to competing pressures of producing effective public relations, dealing with the minutiae of financial management, weathering inspections and ensuring the existence of paper trails for auditors. (Some of this is documented in a detailed case study in Dadds (1995) and in cross-school research by Hargreaves (1994).)

Perhaps we just think are all pushing at the same door when in fact we are pushing at different ones. It is hardly surprising that the widespread welcome for partnership goes with a considerable ambiguity about what the term might mean. This ambiguity is not surprising, because 'partnership' is a generous term. It is used to cover a myriad of different relationships and it encompasses a wide range of meanings, including other generous terms such as 'cooperation', 'participation' and 'collaboration', and more parsimonious ones such as 'teamwork', 'joint working', 'co-ownership' and 'multi-agency working', all of which are themselves somewhat ambiguous.[1] The term 'partnership' can be used to indicate an equal share of power, or, on the contrary, it can assign control to one partner and the provision of energy, time, money and so on to the other. Different metaphors that are used to describe partnership point to the range of understandings possible. One well known metaphor is the body, where there is a head, a stomach, limbs and so on, all of which need each other but have different degrees of control and status. Another is the metaphor of the 'partnership of horse and rider'. These stand in contrast to metaphors of a hive, a family, a marriage or a cooperative business venture. Within education, the idea of a teacher–parent partnership has been shown to carry very different meanings to teachers and parents in relation to power and participation: teachers have often assumed they need to tell parents how to help; parents have often assumed they need to explain to teachers what their children need (Bastiani 1989; Vincent 1996; Crozier 1998; Wolfendale and Bastiani 2000).

The ambiguity surrounding 'partnership' can be productive if it brings people with broadly similar motives together. But if the underlying motives conflict, then at some point such conflicts may need to be recognized and confronted in relation to issues of ownership, control, accountability and prioritization – or there is a risk of disaster in whatever enterprise is being carried out.[2]

So why do educators consult and get into partnership? What are the motives for doing it? Partnership may be advocated for reasons based in democratic principles; that is, action ought to be based in consent, consultation and common purpose. Knowledge about what to do will be soundly based only if it has been derived from a variety of perspectives.[3] This book has been giving arguments for the democratic reasons for taking different perspectives into account, and for working 'with' others rather than 'on' or even 'for' them (see Part 1). Clearly, anything that is done in partnership *with* others in a spirit of equality, democracy and solidarity is a matter of social justice, in the sense that in its conduct and outcomes it should lead to a fairness both for individuals and for society as a whole (see Part 1, especially Chapter 4).

Alternatively, reasons may be pragmatic and prudent rather than principled: the driving force is effectiveness rather than values; success is judged in terms of what works. Partnership is advocated because an initiative is more likely to be successful if those implementing it have been partners to it: if they feel they have 'ownership'. Funding requirements may include the development of partnerships: partnership pays. It may also be a matter of survival, akin to a business merger or takeover (Bridges and Husbands 1996; Wilson and Charlton 1997).

Of course, motives for getting into partnership are likely to be mixed, and the different partners may well have different views of the main motive. The collection of articles by Bridges and Husbands (1996: 5) discusses the 'combination of educational and social idealism with political and economic realism' that impels schools towards collaborating with each other, in order to survive and to be effective in terms of their own educational values. This situation continues. Idealistic motives continue to have a hold: about working with, rather than working on, and power sharing. These motives underlie partnerships for justice.

Partnerships for justice: consulting and conversing

Recognizing inequalities and differences

There is an obvious difficulty about setting up partnerships for justice. They are set up precisely in order to draw on systematic, structural differences in perspective, including recognition of ways in which lack of equality structures the argument. So different perspectives on, and relationships to, power and status are inescapable. Such partnerships could be described as equal in the sense that all the partners are equal in humanity, in deserving respect, but they could just as well be described as rooted in inequality, in that the partners are there precisely because there is an imbalance in power, in status, in material or cultural capital, in access to other forms of power and so on. So, paradoxically, there is a need to recognize difference, including inequalities that matter, in order to establish partnerships for justice: partnerships that are fair, equitable and just.

The usual story is that there are three tenets that would hold in relation to the practice of collaboration. Discussion should (a) take place between people who are considered equals, and (b) be open and honest. (c) As a result of open and honest discussion it will be possible to reach a consensus – or at least a majority agreement – about the enterprise, and provide everyone with an agreed, rational basis for action.

Well, who could disagree? These orthodox suggestions are persuasive and attractive. The reasons why the suggestions are persuasive stem from their emphasis on values related to equality, justice and the possibility of rational, collective action. The problem lies with the way these suggestions are usually interpreted – that a collaborative group can behave as equals in the public space. That is, it assumes that there is a sharp split between people in their day-to-day roles, with all their differences of power, status, normal modes of argument and interaction, and the same people in a public space, where they are equals in respect of argument and rational decision-making. For instance, Postlethwaite and Haggarty (1998: 334) assert that their role as university lecturers in their collaboration with schoolteachers was as 'equal members of the group, engaging in debate about the issues'. They may have been right in their perception. But other studies show that, if so, they were fortunate. Of course, disappointments and difficulties are often more easily discussed with the benefit of hindsight and distance. As Julie Kniskern (2000: 59–60) states in her self-study of a development project she helped to set up, one devised to create a collaboration between university and schools in Manitoba:

> There were significant power relationships that militated against on-going communication [a year after the project was set up] . . . I took the failure of this project very personally and for a long time I could not talk or write about it. Now that I have written about it, I am able to see the factors that contributed to its failure.

These factors are not confined to one country or culture. Similar disappointments and difficulties faced Deborah Chetcuti in the University of Malta (Chetcuti 2000) and Kwame Akyeampong and J. G. Ampiah in the University of Cape Coast, Ghana (Sayed *et al.* 2000).

What is to be done? What ways can be found to use differences in equalities for equity and justice? What ways can be found to go beyond liberal hopes of leaving power at the door, which I have long argued are a fantasy. In a discussion of how action research can become seen by teachers as a management tool, I asked: 'Is one person's co-operation and consensus another's coercion and constraint?' (Griffiths 1990: 39). The question had been posed in the context of my working alongside a first-grade teacher in Maine, carrying out a successful piece of classroom based action research together (it has now had a significant long-term impact over a decade). I was comparing its success to that of a state-wide attempt to introduce cooperative working in Maine (I observed little impact at classroom level then or subsequently).

Similar reflections by Bridget Somekh (1994) in England and Melanie Walker in South Africa point to the importance of acknowledging the complexities of power. As Walker (1997: 139) writes, 'The notion of collaboration from different spaces and across different discourses [is] a collaboration recognizably criss-crossed by lines of power rather than some patronizing notion of "equality".' It appears that ways must be found to be less squeamish about acknowledging the effects of power and its distribution and ways of mitigating this in terms of getting real conversation and consultation going. Fortunately, a number of accounts are emerging that focus on specific partnerships, the delights and tensions of the processes and how they result in both triumphs and tragedies along the way. These accounts give us reason to be optimistic that it is possible to realize the values related to equity, justice and the possibilities of rational, collective action – and, indeed, make it more likely by combining an equality of respect for the other *as* other with an equality of proper humility about the inescapability of all perspectives being partial. They point to the importance of acknowledging differences of power, status, language, style and purpose, and building up strategies to mitigate them. A particularly useful example is a detailed investigation by participants in a six-year, longitudinal collaboration, a professional development partnership of some schools with Ohio State University (Johnston *et al.* 1997). The report itself is a collaborative piece of writing, albeit one for which the overall coordinator of the project, Marilyn Johnston, must (and does) take prime responsibility. The contributors reflect on their differences and problems as well as on their common ground and their considerable successes. Similarly, careful, honest reports, sensitive to the variety of perspectives, have been compiled on a partnership in Illinois, USA (Clift *et al.* 2000) and on others in Cambridge, England (Dadds 1995; James and Worrall 2000).

What emerges from all these accounts is the way the personal and professional cannot be separated for the people involved in partnerships.[4] The reports of successful partnerships show that all concerned bring their whole selves to the projects: their passions and vulnerabilities, personal strengths and idiosyncrasies, social and family relations, ambitions and ideals. And it is this that gives us a clue about what makes them work (and not). It is normal for human beings to deal with individual differences. It is also normal for human beings to live with power imbalances; we routinely cooperate with people who are unequal in all kinds of ways. Consider family life, neighbours, adults at work, community groups and school classrooms. They are marked by differences of status, age, class, gender, race and sexuality. All human beings act from a mixture of self-interest and altruism. So human beings have found a number of ways of dealing with all this. They include conviviality, reciprocity and a huge range of forms of communication. They also recognize that relationships are mortal (Clift *et al.* 2000): are born, go through changes and die, and need care and nurturing over that time.

Conviviality

One of our local headteachers, who is known for her skills in making and keeping partnerships, is also known for the excellence of the cakes produced in meetings at her school. It is no accident that successful partnerships are cemented with food and informality. Conviviality helps to bring people together, and to see each other as individuals rather than just as professional role holders. They can enjoy meeting as fellow human beings and feel valued for themselves. This is what Paulo Freire meant by his comment, 'First we eat, and then we do the work.'[5]

Research evidence confirms the role of conviviality (Chang-Wells and Wells 1997; Wilson and Charlton 1997; Clift *et al.* 2000). Two to three years after we had last seen each other, I visited members of the Nottingham Group for Social Justice, my partners on the Fairness Project (see Chapter 6), to see what, if anything, we might do now about carrying the project into a second phase. I discovered (to my surprise) just how significant conviviality had been to them. I had expected that my colleagues would remember something of the meetings and decisions we had made, if not the details. So I was very interested to notice how memories of the project were imbued with vivid memories of personal feelings about shared events. (Mine were too.) This was especially striking given the explicit pragmatic purpose of the interview: to take stock and decide on the next practical step. And also given the fact that these colleagues are all busy and task-oriented.

The members of the group remembered lunch, individual people and feelings of vulnerability or pride. They fitted all this into the continuing complex of ways in which they continue to work for social justice. We had worked better together because we gave ourselves the opportunity to be convivial in pleasant surroundings. We also worked better because we acknowledged that each one of us had our own 'life story' or 'path' that had to be taken into account when thinking where to go next. Here are two representative comments:

> I remember coming to the university, and having a really good meal! [Laughter] . . . Although I was worried about being with all these intelligent people, clever people [the meal] made me feel comfortable . . . It was very calm . . . It was a nice day. It was a lovely sunny day. (Carol)

> I can remember the university, the two days we had at the university, discussing a curriculum set for social justice . . . It's not a detailed memory. I can remember sitting and having the lunch. [Laughter] . . . A big window. We were sitting in a room and talking to each other. A really lovely window! . . . What I do remember are the feelings and the emotions that were there, and the people who had their different, in a way, life stories about where they were at. (Prakash)

Reciprocity

The importance of reciprocity is well understood in ordinary human relationships. Mutual gift giving and the exchange of favours are as central to human life as conviviality. Indeed, conviviality provides the occasion for some of it. It is important to see that reciprocity is not served well by all parties giving the same gifts or favours. It works on the assumption that different partners to a relationship bring different strengths, needs, abilities and ways of making others feel delighted or fulfilled. Partnership works well when this is acknowledged and built in. My colleague alluded to some of this in the second e-mail I quoted in the introductory section. She points out how all the participants benefit from the contributions of the others. This depends on them being different: school teacher, school pupil, student teacher, teacher educator, as well as Indian and English. The partnership thrives precisely because there is the possibility of a reciprocal exchange of benefits.

The importance of reciprocity is that it can acknowledge inequalities at the same time as using them for the mutual benefit of all partners. Reciprocity is rarely discussed in relation to partnerships, probably because an emphasis on 'equality as sameness' leads to a desire that everyone should get the same benefits as everyone else. Thus, when I was writing an academic paper about my work with Carol Davies, the journal referee demanded that she contribute some writing. This would have been a burden for her (though writing our book for teachers was not). What is more, it would not have contributed to her career as it would to mine. We were able to explain this to the editor, because we were clear about the different benefits each of us gained from our partnership over the years (Griffiths and Davies 1995: 9–11). Other accounts of long-term partnerships point to similar exchanges (Dadds 1995; Cockburn 1998; James and Worrall 2000; McTaggart *et al.* 1997).

Rich forms of communication

Here is Robin Richardson explaining something of how he worked to establish an equal opportunities policy in Berkshire nearly 20 years ago. It was established successfully, surviving for years, despite his departure and despite political changes in local and central government.

> There needs to be the exhausting – and yes, stressful, painful and tearful – process of real consultation, real negotiation: drafting committees, discussion papers, public meetings, press releases and coverage, one-day conferences, specialist seminars, serious research, deputations, petitions, minuted resolutions, formal submissions; and argument, argument, argument much of it impassioned and angry.
>
> (Richardson 1989: 172–3)

Anyone familiar with Richardson's work would know he should have added to the list of forms of language at least the following: stories, anecdotes, jokes, parables, autobiography, verse and satire.

Partnerships are too often approached as if they take place in seminar rooms where polite, abstract, dispassionate, rational discussion is the norm. But human beings are passionate and they care about their work. They also have the full riches of language at their disposal. Most of us are good at switching register and genre in ordinary life. We can bring these skills to partnerships.

Different forms of language are suited to different purposes and contexts. Conversely, the form of language best suited for one kind of knowledge, practice and action will not necessarily be the best language for another (Lyotard 1984). We may want to communicate information but we also want to gain wisdom, tell stories and cultivate our sense of ourselves in relation to our skills and pleasures, dreams and deeds. The ubiquitous bullet point and the formal report have their place. So do academic prose replete with references, anecdotes in newspapers, polemic and, most especially, the oral culture of meetings, presentations and workshops. There are class, culture or gender preferences about forms of language and about ground rules of conversations (Tannen 1992, 1995). Moreover, teachers often feel uncomfortable with the technical language of academics.

Partnerships need to be alert to the variety of language that will help them work. Words need to be chosen carefully. They may need to convey information or argument in plain dry prose. Equally, they may need to express passionate feelings about the purposes of the partnership. At a conference, the education philosopher Pádraig Hogan described what he has learnt from teaching geography to disaffected adolescents in terms of 'responding to the deepest yearnings of the human spirit'. He is using the language carefully and precisely to communicate his meaning.

Relationships in progress: change decay and renewal

> Partnerships are mortal, not immortal, and because they can expire at any time they need care, sustenance, and continual reaffirmation of the importance of their existence.
>
> (Clift *et al*. 2000: 105)

Renee Clift and her colleagues wanted to tell the story of their partnership in progress, precisely to challenge the view that once a partnership is set up it is 'enduring, stable and potentially immortal' (Clift *et al*. 2000: 91).

Partnerships are relatively easy to set up. However, after the beginning phase they go into a second phase of consolidation during which the partnership must be carefully nurtured if it is to be maintained. The second phase is much more difficult to manage successfully than the first. It demands maintenance and nurture. Finally, once the consolidation phase is over, and the partnership is thoroughly in place, a decision needs to be made about the longer term. If the partnership has served its purpose, an exit strategy can be devised. Alternatively, the partnership can be drawn on and used over a surprisingly long period. As described in the previous sections, robust partnerships are dependent on rich networks of formal and informal links, as well as on shared goals and agreed ways of working, as the next section shows.

Getting real: working together

Each chapter in Part 2 has a section called 'Getting real'. The purpose is to move from an examination of ideas in general terms – where examples are used to illuminate the theorizing – to a more practical perspective. It is also important to see what practical use can be made of the ideas in specific circumstances: for *real individuals*, with their *specific socio-political positions* (race, class, gender, sexuality and so on), in *particular educational contexts* (classrooms, schools, tertiary institutions) and *in relation to identifiable communities* (their own members, local communities, advisors, universities, national or international networks of educators). This section is not intended to give lots of tips for lessons or policies. Instead, it is intended to inspire and illuminate, by showing the ideas in action, in all their contextual specificity, enacted by real people. It is hoped that these examples will help educators to rethink what they, themselves, might do in their own contexts.

Perspectives on community links in an inner city primary school

'Hillside' is an inner-city primary school that has been successful in fostering good home–school and community–school links. It has a high proportion of children from a Pakistani Muslim background. The head and the teachers on their side, and the community on its side, have worked hard to make sure that the children benefit from their schooling, while remaining at ease with their identity as Muslims of Pakistani heritage. In this the partnership is largely successful. The school knows this, because it asked outsiders to the school to arrange to obtain evidence so that it could improve what it is doing. That evidence shows some of the fine grain of the ongoing process of getting practices and policies – both formal and informal – that work. Provisions for halal dinners had been made at the school, for instance. Successful attempts have been made to recruit teachers and governors who are themselves Pakistani Muslims. There are regular meetings with community leaders. Perspectives from the various partners (children, governors, teachers, the headteacher) show that the school is successful in its aims. They also show the delicate balance that is needed to keep this process working.

The children were asked (by a young adult Pakistani Muslim who was not connected with the school) whether it was easy being a Pakistani Muslim at school. The adult said that the general reaction was a positive one. In fact, some children looked puzzled that she had even asked them this question. They were confident and happy about their identity and felt at ease with combining school life with their distinctive religious and cultural upbringing. The problems they cited revolved mostly around language difficulties. For instance, one boy said: 'If I'm ill or I can't come to school, my mum can't come in and tell them because she has to look after my little brother, and she can't write English and I can't send a letter. My dad comes home too late.'

Most of the children thought their parents were very interested in their schooling. They said things like: 'My mum and dad ask me, "What did you do?" Sometimes I tell them. They say, "Don't be naughty!" ' Or 'My dad says, "I'll come and see your report, and if it is good, we'll be happy".'

In relation to the Muslim children of Pakistani heritage, teachers explained the dilemmas they faced; for instance, in relation to keeping contact with the parents, to PE and swimming lessons and – it was courageous of the teacher to express this – to difference. (The third quotation comes from the Headteacher.)

> The Pakistani Muslim parents that I've met have mostly been dads. I've hardly met any mums. At the formal parents' evenings they haven't spoken to me. I've said hello, and they've come forward and done all the nice things, but they've been in the background. Maybe it is because they don't speak English. I don't know.

> I find it is PE where Pakistani Muslim girls are coming up to me and saying, 'I don't want to do PE this week,' and it's clearly partly about getting changed. It's very hard. I don't really know what to do. They're outnumbered by the white children who don't get it together, families that are a bit chaotic or whatever. There'll usually be as many white girls that don't want to do PE as Muslim girls. Last year I had a little room where they could get changed. I haven't got anywhere I can send them now and it's awkward really.

> In the end we are statutorily required for children to go swimming at the end of Key Stage 2. They have to swim 25 metres which is really tricky if they're not actually in the swimming pool. So in the end our view is that children cannot miss swimming. I know for some of our families that's an unhappy resolution.

> I find it very hard to empathize properly with Muslims, because I find it hard to empathize with anyone whose faith means so much and influences so much of your life. I am an atheist. At my last school there were a lot of 'born again' Christians, and I found it equally hard to see where they were coming from. I just couldn't get my head round it, and it is the same with Islam.

The head and the teachers explained how they approached resolving difficulties. It is significant that they professed themselves keen to evaluate their practice and improve on it, in all areas, not just in relation to the race issues they were being asked about. One teacher said:

> I'm particularly interested in things like how we can move the school from being, really a very good school at managing children who have all sorts of emotional difficulties . . . towards getting greater academic achievement with our children. I don't think our children are achieving as much as they could if we were doing things in a slightly different way.

They make use of what links they have. The Pakistani Muslim teachers are given space to develop and nurture links with the parents, and supported in doing so. The following two quotations are from Pakistani Muslim teachers:

> If a child doesn't come to school I will go to their house to find out why, and they will tell me various reasons. The parents speak to me in confidence. They think I am like their own kith and kin. A mother spoke to me and said, 'You know my husband is a priest, and I cannot send my girl to the swimming pool, because of other people.' So I persuaded her that the child wear leggings, only with consultation with the swimming supervisor, because we have to look at the safety aspect as well. And I gave them the example that my own daughters go swimming and I have a lot of Muslim friends whose daughters go swimming.

> When we invite the parents I'll be there and so will another Pakistani Muslim teacher, to support the parents. They need a chance to talk.

At the same time white teachers work at improving communication.

> Translations are not only important for people who can't speak English. It is a matter of respect that translation should be available for all people whose mother tongue isn't English.

> I signed up for a course at the local college in Urdu, just because I thought it would be really useful even if I just learned 200 words. I'd like to find out a bit more about Islam.

Perhaps it is this level of openness that allows teachers to deal honestly and creatively with what they really feel. The same atheist teacher who explained his problems with religious difference said:

Maybe [my difficulty empathizing with religious people] is why I keep coming back to language, because I can imagine what it would be like. The first school I went to was a school where I couldn't speak the language, so I can imagine what that's like.

Answering back

Each of the chapters in Part 2 has a section called 'Answering back'. I invited seven people to 'answer back' with responses to chapters. The intention is to have more than one perspective on the issues in Part 2 and to keep the thinking about them in process rather than concluded. Some of the contributors have addressed their response to me directly, using the second person 'you'. Others have made a more general response using the third person.

Roy Corden. Ambushed by partnership

It is strange how things can become such an important part of your life without you realizing it. Partnership . . . well . . . it just crept up on me really. At some stage in my life, I cannot recall when, but at some intellectual or emotional crossroads it ambushed me. I am not sure that I put up much of a fight. I must have done. After all, I was fiercely independent. I travelled alone: it was quicker, quieter and remarkably amicable. Decisions were easy, aims and objectives clear and outcomes reached with consummate ease. Until now I have not attempted to analyse what happened or to question why I capitulated so readily. With hindsight I realize that I allowed it to happen for selfish reasons. I found that I could no longer reach my journey's end alone. I needed companions to shield me and to share responsibility. I needed people with knowledge and skills I did not possess. I needed someone else to take the blame if I got lost.

It started that way but, like all good relationships, it has grown stronger until I cannot imagine what it would be like to travel alone again. Of course, the selfish motivation is still there but balanced by altruism and a genuine desire to make a difference, to contribute, to help people to develop quality in their lives, on their terms and according to their perceptions. So I have asked myself how this personal and professional epiphany happened. In seeking an answer I must retrace my steps, go back in time and identify critical moments. In unearthing and sharing these I hope to clarify my own understanding of partnership and explain why I now value it so much.

I was ambushed in 1987. I was commissioned by my Local Education Authority to undertake research into oracy (speaking and listening). This local work later formed part of the National Oracy Project (see Norman 1992). I became a regional project coordinator and for three years worked with 100 teachers in 30 schools. In the chapter, Morwenna has suggested that partnerships can be wonderful and difficult, productive and energizing, powerful and disappointing. My work with teachers in the Oracy Project was all of these things. I experienced the agony and ecstasy of research partnership. The agony came from seeing highly motivated teachers being either restricted in their practice or removed altogether from the project by more powerful others who lacked the same level of conviction or did not have the same vision. But then, as Oscar Wilde suggested, in the one hour of life's misery there are a few magical moments. Here is one I recall.

Morag, a 50-year-old primary school teacher attending a meeting, sits in the auspicious surroundings of a university boardroom. She is surrounded by academics and leading educationalists, from around the world. They have been talking for more than an hour when there is a slight pause in their highbrow and erudite discussion. Morag coughs gently, looks slightly uncomfortable but begins. She looks at a spot somewhere in the distance and suddenly seems unaware of anyone else in the room. She talks about her experience in the project, of what it has meant to her personally and professionally. She speaks softly, unselfconsciously and without hesitation for 10 minutes. Abruptly, but not prematurely, she ends. She has said all she needs to say. There is total silence. The intellectuals are awed. I smile. The personal and professional are inseparable. This is partnership.

Morwenna's argument about the importance of conviviality and reciprocity is a powerful one and is nowhere more apparent than in my current research project (see Corden 2001). This involves teachers working in partnership with colleagues in their own schools, with colleagues from other schools and with me as a university tutor. I believe this to be truly interactive, multilayered partnership. It is interactive because the research requires teachers to observe and critically evaluate each other's practice and to share their findings with others locally, nationally and internationally. It is multilayered because the teachers are so diverse in terms of age, experience, knowledge and expertise. Conviviality pervades the project; without it the research would fail. Mutual trust and respect has to underpin partnership research simply because it brings together people from different perspectives offering a range of strengths. However, because partnership research is interactive and the participants are interdependent, it also exposes people's weaknesses. As I reflect on my experience as an educational researcher, the thing I find most impressive is the total trust placed in me by teachers. I recall Linda, an Oracy Project teacher, saying, 'One of the best things about Roy is that you can tell him about your failures.'

The importance of conviviality and reciprocity has been emphasized, more recently, by my current teacher-researchers (Corden 2001). Central to our work is Vygotsky's notion of the zone of proximal development (ZPD), which suggests that people's independent learning capacity can be enhanced with support from a more knowledgeable other. This has been the guiding principle of our work with children and has led to impressive results. One child epitomized the outcome in her comment: 'I never knew I was this good.'

The teachers said they felt exactly the same way and that I, as the project coordinator, had been scaffolding them in just the same way as they had been scaffolding the children. They were right – but it was not this simple. My role was to inspire and motivate them, and to provide a theoretical platform to underpin their practice. Their role was not only to do the same for their pupils but also to observe, record, analyse and present data. Everyone, including the children, contributed towards a mutually rewarding experience. This is partnership and it is why I am glad I was ambushed.

Notes

1 It is not only educators who live with ambiguity. See Wilson and Charlton (1997) for some definitions in other public and private sector contexts. I have made no attempt to distinguish 'partnership' from 'collaboration', 'cooperation' or 'collaboration' in this chapter.
2 See, for instance, Wilson and Charlton (1997: 24–5).
3 For some purposes the knowledge argument is best distinguished from the democratic actions argument (Griffiths 2000).
4 Note that 'personal' should not be confused with 'private' (Griffiths 1995).
5 This remark was made at a conference and noted by members of the audience. (Melanie Walker, personal communication.)

8   Best practice:
the dynamics of justice

Introduction

My teacher was scolding one of the other children for something I had done.
I remember feeling I had to do the difficult, right thing. I tried to own up,
bravely, I thought. 'Be quiet and sit down!' she snapped. I must have been no
more than five or six and I can still feel the burning injustice of it. Shutting
me up when I had something relevant to say! The unfairness to my class-
mate! The impossibility of doing anything about it. The arrogance of the
powerful.

Mr and Mrs Smith, who ran my junior school, taught me justice by
example. No children in their classes were allowed to feel stupid or humiliated
because they found work difficult. No children were allowed to feel arrogant –
or bored – because they found work easy. I know: I was quick and sharp at
maths (taught by Mr Smith) but slow and clumsy at art and craft (taught by
Mrs Smith). I fell in love with algebra, yes, but also I looked forward eagerly to
the after-school embroidery club. I remember the courtesy accorded to my
classmates who were slower at grasping mathematics. Much later, as a junior
school teacher myself, I went on to teach more children to enjoy both maths
and embroidery.

From experiences like these, I learned about justice and unfairness. The
small unremarkable happenings of an education may teach children lessons
that are unexpectedly lasting. They may become critical incidents in a life,
remembered when much else is forgotten. I could have told an autobiography
of justice and education quite differently of course – much less anecdotally.
My class position, my gender, my race, that my junior school was an all-white
one in an African country: all this is relevant. As is the fact that I was born into
a family of teachers. I could have discussed what material and cultural capital I
inherited and how it was used.

Our actions for justice spring from the persons we are, formed as we are
both by our personal, passionate engagements with other people and by

our position in the large-scale social structures framing our lives. This chapter discusses different ways in which it is possible for individuals to move towards justice: the many ways in which they make history, even if not in circumstances of their own choosing; or, to use Maxine Greene's words, the many ways within which we can perform in the dialectic of freedom (Greene 1988).

Social justice is a verb – with a subject

Action is needed because analysis and understanding are not enough. Nor is empathy. Nor, even, is feeling empowered, without some hope of action and change. Without people taking action, there is no hope of getting more fairness into educational practices. In other words, social justice is a verb. Furthermore, it is an active verb, not a passive one. It must have a subject: justice does not *get done* unless *somebody does* it (see Chapter 4).

Someone has to do it. It would be more accurate to say: some people have to do it. Even individual actions are taken in a social context, and, usually, they are done with others. Children are fed stories of heroes, from the Viking heroes slaying monsters through exemplary righters of wrongs (Emmeline Pankhurst, Mary Seacole, Martin Luther King) to the superheroes of today's comics (Warner 1994). Children are misled by these stories. Changes happen and, no doubt, occasionally it is a hero who makes them happen. Even then, it is rarely alone. As Bertoldt Brecht put it in a poem:

> Young Alexander conquered India.
> Was he alone?
> Caesar beat the Gauls.
> Did he not even have a cook with him?

Rather than endless stories of heroes fighting single-handed, a better exemplar would be found in Aesop's fable of the mice freeing the lion by nibbling through the net. Just as each mouse could only nibble through some small part of the net, but between them, they could make a big hole, so changes require cooperation from others. We are mice rather than lions. Most heroes are not superheroes and the factual (as opposed to the fictional) ones usually need other people – as did Pankhurst, Seacole and King. In the fable, one mouse enlisted the help of the others. Furthermore, the mouse who started it all had, unlike most mice, conversed with a lion. So one of the morals to be drawn from the fable is that change is started by a specific, complex individual with her specific, complex, personal history.

Whether an action is started by one person (who needs others to join in) or whether it is started by a collective (see Chapters 7 and 9), the individuals who are joining in do so as individuals, with their own strengths and weaknesses, preferences, histories and socio-political position. The self or selves that start the actions are each marked by their history and by their own individual responses to that history. They are marked by their changing relationship to their social and political status (gender, race, sexuality and so on). As I have argued elsewhere (Griffiths 1995), we are, each of us, a patchwork self in which new patches join, adjoin or obscure what is already there. It is a patchwork, made over time, of patches upon patches, continually worked over, but with no possibility of being thrown out or erased in order to start afresh.

A significance of patchwork for social justice is the effect on action. Some of the patchwork was made out of the alliances we have formed, the groups with which we have identified, or from which we have been rejected, or which we have resisted joining. As Stuart Hall has pointed out, we never identify 100 per cent with any group.[1] It is either 80 per cent because the individual feels a bit different from the others, or 120 per cent because she tells herself that she is just the same as all of them (which, of course, she cannot be). Each individual can draw on a variety of patches. An individual self is always part of more than one 'we'. She can make different alliances at different times. So, probably, her alliances shift according to context and circumstance, and she has some freedom to choose which ones to espouse.

Acting reflectively, acting up

There is more than one way to make things change for the better. In this section, I draw attention to two of them: reflective action and playful – including naughty – action. Both kinds are intelligent, responsive and rational. In saying this, I am calling action 'intelligent, responsive and rational' where the person doing it (a) understands the context, (b) wants to do something about it and (c) does it, and where (d) the action is coherent with most other actions she does.

Reflective actions

Reflective action is best understood as taking place within reflective cycles (or action research, or self-study cycles). A situation is assessed. If something needs to be done, it is – and the result is evaluated. The situation can then be reassessed to see if anything else needs to be done. These kinds of actions are straightforwardly rational. They are planned, predictable, judged against initial objectives; reflective practitioners (or action researchers) have clear aims and objectives, are sensible and intelligent, and abide by codes of value. They are also responsive to changing circumstances, in that their aims and objectives can – and usually do – alter over the course of several cycles.

'Reflective practice' sounds as if it might simply be thinking about what you do. At the simplest level it is. But I am using it more precisely than that, in a sense ultimately derived from Dewey's ideas about it (Dewey 1916). To be precise, reflective action can be recognized by the following descriptions. First, it is action taken in relation to the agent's own situation. Second, reflection and action are tightly interlinked. To use Schon's well known formulation, it includes both reflection-in-action and reflection-on-action (Schon 1983). That is, it refers to the kind of concentration and intelligence needed at the time and also to thinking afterwards about what happened. Third, the reflection-on-action includes paying attention to wider, relevant theorizing by others.

For this reason reflective action is well suited to improving social justice. It is a way of linking strategic actions at both local and global levels and, similarly, at personal and structural levels. That is, it is a way of responding to situations taking into account *both* the particular and the personal *and* the social, political and economic order.

Figure 8.1 shows how reflective action proceeds by doing something about a situation, and how it allows for making mistakes. There are three cycles, all going on simultaneously. In Figure 8.1 they are shown as nested, but a three-dimensional model would be more accurate. As portrayed here, reflection-in-action is the innermost cycle of the diagram (termed 'monitoring', to indicate that it is going on from moment to moment). But it links directly with the middle cycle, short-term reflection-on-action (termed 'evaluation' to indicate that it takes place soon after the action). The outermost cycle includes the long-term reflections-on-actions. This is the cycle in which links are made

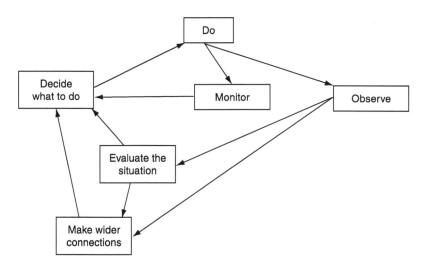

Figure 8.1 A model of reflective action

with larger issues, theories and principles and with similar actions going on in other similar contexts.

Acting up

Playful actions are less obviously rational than reflective ones. Perhaps this is because we are all so dominated by the language of performance indicators, strategic plans and missions, so characteristic of managerialism. However, just because managerialism can claim to be rational, that is no reason to think that it is the only form of rationality. Human beings – rational animals – are also spontaneous, creative, disruptive, clever and principled. They understand the rules but they can push them intentionally, often having fun as they do it – and sometimes enjoying being naughty. Naughty children are said to be acting up. They are indeed acting, in the sense that they are doing something freely in response to a situation. Such actions can be gleeful: expressive of self but ultimately doing nothing more than making a tedious situation more fun. (The stories told by Edwin (Chapter 1) and Sharon (Chapter 4) include such actions.) Playful actions – including naughty ones – are also a creative and rational way of responding to a situation to improve the justice in it.

Playful actions draw on the delights and difficulties of patchwork selves. They allow for different patches to be expressed, even if that goes against the norms of another patch. Maria Lugones has helpfully referred to this switching between parts of oneself as 'world travelling'. Although I would criticize and extend her description (Griffiths 1999), I find her analysis very useful. Like her, I recommend travelling (moving between patches) in the spirit of spontaneity, creativity and disruption – in short, playfully. Lugones (1989: 275) writes: 'I recommend this wilful exercise, which I call "'world'-travelling", and I also recommend that the wilful exercise be animated by an attitude that I describe as playful.' Lugones advocates playfulness as an attitude. She describes playfulness as fun, not necessarily rule-governed, as undertaken in a spirit of 'openness to surprise', to 'being a fool', to 'not worrying about competence, not being self-important, not taking norms as sacred and finding ambiguity and double edges a source of wisdom and delight' (Lugones 1989: 288). However, as she also points out, there is a double edge to play and naughtiness. Children are sometimes naughty in response to intolerable situations. The same is true for anyone finding themselves caught up in unfair situations. Play, especially naughty play, can spring from pain and difficulty, and is one way of dealing with them.

There are a number of ways of playing. Here is one way of mapping and describing them.

- *Role play and playing with stereotypes.* Travelling between worlds. Activating stereotypes – so playing the role, but knowing you are doing it and that you need not. Reclaiming them. Refusing them. Flouting the rules. Trespassing beyond the boundaries, and then claiming the space.

- *Laughter*. Irony. Playing the fool. Playing tricks. Political jokes. Refusing to take authority seriously.
- *Imagination*. Double-vision: seeing things from two perspectives, at least. Thinking of ways of playing one persona against another. Entertaining forbidden fantasies. Imaginative performances. Dreaming up and doing the unexpected.

This is only a rough mapping, intended to open up the understanding. I do not want to place the dead hand of category on what is, or ought to be – and, indeed, must be – fluid, unfixed, imaginative and creative. Instead, it can be seen how these possibilities are realized in particular examples. For instance, consider Fatima Mernissi's wonderful evocation of harem life in Morocco in the 1940s, *Dreams of Trespass*, and her education into the power of play, creativity – and naughtiness.

Mernissi is a feminist, Islamic scholar, world famous for books on democracy, the veil and women rulers in Islamic history. Her narrative of childhood is vivid, affectionate, political, feminist – and full of lessons on naughtiness. Her mother gave her some of these with the help of her own mother, Grandmother Yasmina. Her mother had 'always rejected male superiority, as nonsense and totally anti-Muslim – "Allah made us all equal," she would say' (Mernissi 1994: 9). She was worried when her little girl merely admired her cousin when he 'staged his mutinies against the grownups', and let him do her rebelling for her. The little girl was told by her mother, 'You have to learn to scream and protest, just the way you learned to walk and talk. Crying when you are insulted is like asking for more. She was so worried that I would grow up to be an obsequious woman that she consulted Grandmother Yasmina, known to be incomparable at staging confrontations' (Mernissi 1994: 9). These confrontations were playful and political as well as dangerous. 'What always saved Yasmina was the fact that she made Grandfather laugh' (Mernissi 1994: 30–1), even though she asserted her wish to climb trees, go swimming, do acrobatics and name the farm peacock Farouk after the Egyptian king who had unjustly divorced his wife (Mernissi 1994: 151–3):

> Yasmina said having two masters was better than one, because if you could not get permission from one master you could always turn to the other . . . The more masters one had, the more freedom and the more fun . . . 'Figuring out who has *sulta* [authority] over you is the first step,' said Yasmina. 'That information is basic. But after that, you need to shuffle the cards, confuse the roles. That is the interesting

part. Life is a game. Look at it that way, and you can laugh at the whole thing.'

(Mernissi 1994: 151–3)

Embroidery was another lesson in dreaming and getting freedom. The traditional women in the harem – led by the most senior woman, Grandmother Mani – believed that all embroidery should be of the tedious traditional kind. They disapproved of modern designs which, explains Mernissi (1994: 209), 'were pure fun, meant for personal enjoyment'. But she makes it clear that the traditionalists were right to see danger in the modern designs, which were symbolic of more than personal enjoyment. It was not by chance that the modernists used the freedom of 'unexpected designs and strange colour combinations' (Mernissi 1994: 209) to stitch birds with wings spread in full flight. The less powerful of the modernist women had to hide when embroidering their birds. But, as her favourite among them, Aunt Habiba, told her:

> The main thing for the powerless is to have a dream ... Your Grandmother Yasmina's dream was that she was a special creature, and no one has ever been able to make her believe otherwise ... Your mother has wings inside, too, and your father flies with her whenever he can.

(Mernissi 1994: 214–15)

Play and the possibilities of play can spring from the ambiguities and double vision of injustice. This is a difficult balancing act, carried out on the edges of dominant worlds, but one that has a chance of transforming an unjust situation. It is a form of action for justice.

Success and failure

The discussion of action began with a reference to storybook heroes. I pointed out that storybooks may mislead us about the nature of a hero. They may also mislead us with respect to the kinds of endings to expect – especially in the West.

The stories told about struggles for justice may be told as romantic tales, with the narrator as hero, overcoming obstacles by keeping her wits about her and also hoping for a bit of luck. The idea has a hold, even though there can be few adults who easily believe in an ending where anyone lived happily ever after. On the other hand, the stories could be told as being more like one of the Arabian Nights stories, where good and evil exist but the story is not one of the triumph of one or the other. Good and evil appear as significant factors in lives, and are worth struggling with, but the struggle never ends. Nobody lives happily ever after – but then again, neither is any tragedy final. Each story is a tale of neither triumph nor ruin, but of an in-between. This seems to me to be not only closer to experience but also more hopeful. You never win, but then again you never lose either.

However, it is still important to be able to recognize success. The issue becomes: what would count as progress? How would you know if the struggle for justice is successful? At one extreme is the model of the long revolution, in which progress is seen as linear, forward and cumulative, despite many setbacks. Against this is a model in which there can be no progress, only struggle, which is worthwhile in itself. There are other models that are non-cumulative, often expressed in metaphors such as: the underground growth of rhizomes or of mushrooms; border skirmishes and guerrilla warfare; and wire fences that can be pushed down only at the expense of another section of the fence springing up, and so are obstructive but not impassable.

However success is conceptualized, and however the story is told, it is surely important to tell stories of struggles for justice. And it is surely important to celebrate achievements, for that is what keeps us all going.

Getting real: learning new moves

Each chapter in Part 2 has a section called 'Getting real'. The purpose is to move from an examination of ideas in general terms – where examples are used to illuminate the theorizing – to a more practical perspective. It is also important to see what practical use can be made of the ideas in specific circumstances: for *real individuals*, with their *specific socio-political positions* (race, class, gender, sexuality and so on), in *particular educational contexts* (classrooms, schools, tertiary institutions) and *in relation to identifiable communities* (their own members, local communities, advisors, universities, national or international networks of educators). This section is not intended to give lots of tips for lessons or policies. Instead, it is intended to inspire and illuminate, by showing the ideas in action, in all their contextual specificity, enacted by real people. It is hoped that these examples will help educators to rethink what they, themselves, might do in their own contexts.

Racial equality policy in a school with a large majority of white children and teachers

Freya had recently moved from a primary school in the inner city, where there was a very mixed intake of children, from the perspectives of both race and social class. Her new school was much more homogeneous, in a predominantly white suburb of the city. There were about eight minority ethnic children and one minority ethnic teacher in a school of about 250 pupils. She set about constructing a policy that would include issues of race, including bullying and harassment. It was to be a long and careful process. It took three years for the policy to be completed and put into place. Here she is describing how matters stood when she started.

It is hard, because I'm starting so many miles back from where I've ever been. For instance, I said to them, 'Are we doing any spring festivals?' They're doing Easter. And Eid is going to be in the spring this year! I've done Ramadan in my assembly. Three Muslim pupils who are in the juniors did the assembly. It was brilliant! And then the headteacher followed that up.

This is how it happened. I went to the three pupils, and said – because I know a lot, and I had already talked to them, 'I have to do "pilgrimage" with my kids. And I want to do it about Muslims going to Mecca.' Then Nasreen brought in some pictures. Then, because they had brought in the pictures, I said, 'Would you want to help?' They were so pleased! They went and told the headteacher, 'We're going to teach the children!' Then we talked about fasting with my class. My kids were amazed. These three girls don't do it, but I explained that lots of kids at my old school in the same city would be doing it. It was easier there because there were lots of children that did it, and dinner time was geared to help them.

'When are we going to be doing this again? When are we going to be teaching the children?' the three of them kept saying to me. So I said, 'What about an Assembly?' 'Oooh! Ask the Headteacher!' The next day they had made me a big Eid banner. In came clothes, and all sorts. Then it was, 'Well, what are we going to say?' So they brought in a book for me. They brought in some bits from the Koran. Saeeda, Nasreen's older sister, read bits out. 'That's lovely, Saeeda. Would you like to read that out in assembly?' I said. 'Oh, yes!' I thought she would say, 'no,' but she said 'yes'.

I said that I would talk a bit about what Islam is and what being a Muslim is. I wrote something, and I said, 'I want you to tell me if you are happy with what I am saying.' They were. So that is how we did the assembly.

It was really good. When we asked, 'Are there any questions?' the kids asked questions. We stopped it when the last question was, 'Are you allowed to choose your own boyfriend?' 'I think they're just a little young at the moment, and anyway the next class is due to start any minute,' I said at that point. It was lovely. It went really well.

Making progress on gender issues

Elizabeth[2] is the deputy head of a secondary school. She finds it difficult to persuade staff to take equal opportunities as a priority, even where there is good will, because of the pressures of other initiatives: 'We've got eyes rolled to heaven and – almost, "Don't you think we've got enough on without doing this as well?" So I think things are working as a sort of drip drip factor.' She goes on to describe how this 'drip drip factor' works. One example is a gender survey she has conducted with Year 10 pupils, every year for the past three years.

We'd done the picnic tables in the past, because one of the things they had said previously was about the areas of the school which are 'girl-friendly' or 'boy-friendly'. They said there's nothing for the girls to do at lunchtime. There are plenty of spaces for the boys to play football – and for the girls who want to play football. But there aren't the spaces for the girls who want to socialize. So now we've got a few more benches and picnic tables round and about.

Another of the things that has come out of it was about sanctions. When we first did the survey, there were certainly a lot more boys getting detentions than girls. When we analysed why, it tended to be not so much the disobedience – eating in school, or things like that – but handing in homework. It wasn't so much their not having done their homework: it was about handing it in. Girls who didn't hand in their homework went to see the member of staff, simpered and said, 'I'm ever so sorry!' 'Oh, bring it in with you tomorrow.' Whereas the boys just didn't do anything. So we had a bit of assertiveness training, and said to the boys, 'Look, if you haven't done your homework, this is how to deal with it.' I think that helped a little bit. But also it brought up the whole area of kids meeting deadlines. It was about handing in homework, but it was more important when it got to things like coursework. It was the ability to work, and to organize their work.

We have set a lunchtime workroom where people can just go and work. Or they can be sent to do work by a member of staff if the homework hasn't been done, rather than banging them into detention. 'OK, go to the workroom tomorrow and do the work and bring it to me in the afternoon.' It's an area where, if pupils are going out at night, they can just go and do their work. We have tried to divorce that from detention. So we are not sending them instead of a detention, or seeing it as another form of detention, but as a way of avoiding having a school detention. It is now beginning to work. When you set these things up there are always teething troubles. Now, we've done it about two terms – this is the third term – it's beginning to work as we think it should be working. We've got a review to see how it's gone this term. The workroom is open every day from about half past one to quarter past two and it's staffed. We've cut detention down to twice a week because of it. Before, the vast majority of teachers were going in to class: 'You haven't done your work. All right, go and do it today in detention.' It was sending out the wrong sort of messages.

Our boys underachieve, as boys do nationally, but ours do not do so to the extent which some schools are reporting.

Answering back

Each of the chapters in Part 2 has a section called 'Answering back'. I invited seven people to 'answer back' with responses to chapters. The intention is to have more than one perspective on each of the issues in Part 2 and to keep the thinking about them in process rather than concluded. Some of the contributors have addressed their response to me directly, using the second person 'you'. Others have made a more general response using the third person.

Melanie Walker. 'We make the road by walking'

I was intrigued by your opening to this chapter, in which you recount a personal experience of unfairness in school. I liked the way you pointed from the start to the importance of taking into account how each and every person (or child) is enabled to flourish in education, particularly formal education settings, which still seem to me to be something of a black box in relation to our understandings of how our principles of justice translate into action. (Although there are some compelling examples we can draw on and learn from; for example, your collaboration with Carol Davies around fairness in her primary school classroom, and James Beane and Michael Apple's stories of democratic schools, to take just two.) As you say, our little and big autobiographical experiences build over time into patterns and shapes, what we take ourselves to be and what we believe ourselves able to do.

Drawing on my own South African experiences, this points to how children schooled under the grossly unequal system of Bantu education were taught to see themselves only as unskilled labourers, and for the 'lucky' few perhaps as teachers or nurses or factory workers. Thus, in the large-scale social structure of apartheid and patriarchy, individual lives were shaped – black in relation to white, men in relation to women, rich in relation to poor – and choices and aspirations deformed for the many, all in and through the tiny and big details of everyday lives at home, in communities and at schools.

So, yes, social justice is and must be a verb as well as a noun, principles as well as action. On the whole, though, I think that we often prefer to describe or critique the world as it is and are less successful in thinking about how our actions today build an educational world of tomorrow. In South Africa, in a three-year teacher development project in which I worked with black primary school teachers, I used to think of this as building the schools (and the citizens) of tomorrow today. At least when we try to act on our principles of justice (schools of tomorrow) we are faced with the gap between our theories and our practices (trying to work in schools as they are today). The gap is a hard one but also helps us to see the moments and possibilities for something different, more rather than less just. I am not at all sure that we can do this without acting, or researching action.

By the way, when I was teacher in Cape Town in the 1980s we used a version of Brecht's poem as a teaching resource. It was rewritten by a teacher, Carohn Cornell, as 'Who Built Cape Town?' We used poetry and stories a lot, not just in teaching English, but also for subjects like history, to try to show how ordinary people also made the world. Poetry and stories were always a compelling way to point to injustice in the world, injustices mirrored in the lives of the children we taught, so that we were able as teachers to prise open taken-for-granted assumptions about poverty and fairness. As you say, someone has to do it (social justice) and perhaps it was something about the obvious unfairness of how Cape Town worked that led many teachers, black and white, to work for educational and social change.

But what was also apparent in our struggles for change was the gap between our democratic ideas and what we did in classrooms. Often teachers who were strongly committed to democratic organizations were also the same teachers who did not prepare lessons properly or who unreflectively used corporal punishment as a disciplinary weapon. Organizations were seen as the way to change and actions in classroom something of a distraction! I struggled a lot with this because I thought my work in classrooms was important and could make some kind of difference to students' lives. But was the work I was doing with students and later with black teachers just about gilding gutter education, or did it contain at least moments of equity and transformation? And how could I/we know?

I think what I am trying to get at here is how we make judgements about the justice effects of our actions. Social justice, as your opening story suggests, must be for individual flourishing and collective solidarities, the one with the other. But how do we know what takes us closer to justice rather than further away? My friend and colleague, Elaine Unterhalter, puts this very well when she talks of the need for a theory or principles of justice that enable us to adjudicate between our actions so that we can say this action is more just than that. I rather think, without wanting to be frivolous by switching from big struggles against apartheid to a fable about lions and mice, that the mice in the fable you recount must have had a theory in mind, a broader goal against which they could judge and evaluate the effectiveness or justice of their actions. While the work started with the action of one mouse, and then required collaboration, it was action towards a particular end, freedom. So that seems to be another important lesson (or moral) to draw from this story. Not only patchwork selves, then, but also patchwork actions in which the individual pieces of cloth, however bright and lively, are just that, bits of cloth. Only when we stitch the pieces (our actions) together to make a quilt do the patterns emerge and transform the pieces into something new; we need to know what we are trying to make and to be able to judge whether we have made it well.

Most of us will probably experience unfairness in our lives at some point, and these experiences are resources for our own learning and a stimulus for some of us to act for justice in our own situation. But there is also the unfairness we do not see, because we lack the frames to understand it. So we might experience gender unfairness as women in academic life without understanding or even seeing the inequities. We might as racially privileged individuals fail to see racial unfairness in our society, and even in our own actions. And this is not about how much education we have or don't have. Education teaches stuff but not everything. Our patchwork selves will include blind spots and privileged places, so we need the linkages of action and adjudicating social justice theories. A good example of this was a report on a murder trial involving several Ethiopian witnesses. The judge at the Old Bailey told the jury:

> When a lot of witnesses give evidence in a case that is going to take a little time I try to pencil a description. I try to bring them back to you when I sum up. It was quite difficult in this case with the Ethiopian witnesses because you may think they all looked rather similar and it was difficult to find any distinguishing features.

According to an observer quoted in the report:

> The remark appeared to fall like a stone and people lowered their eyes in embarrassment. Many of the witnesses could not have been more dissimilar. Some were tall, some short, some had beards, some were women.
>
> (*Guardian* 29 February 2000)

The judge, an 'educated' man, just did not 'see' the people in front of him, nor was he aware of the injustice of his remarks. But in this small example, we see injustice being reproduced and remade on a daily basis in and through talk and action, set ironically in this case in a place that is supposed to be for justice!

While I think you put the case for reflective action very well, I still think it is extraordinarily complicated to practise the linkages you describe – the particular and the structural. The linkages may well be clear in one's head but less so and more complicated in action! This is why I was so taken by the action research project that Britt-Marie Berge and Hildur Ve (2000) write about in Sweden, in which they come up with the idea of 'moments of equity', in which there is recognizable progress towards gender equity, and 'moments of normalization', which signal resistances to changed gender practices and relationships – gender advance and gender retreat. This seems more doable. You talk of this in a similar way as stories of 'neither triumph or ruin, but of an in between', neither unambiguously winning nor losing. Coming back yet again to my earlier point, it was important in this action research project that participants had an 'adjudicating' theory to evaluate the action of teachers in schools, in this case a theory about gender justice.

Finally, I love the way you weave stories through your text, in this case stories of 'travelling' and 'playing'. I am fascinated by your rough mapping of ways of playing and would like more examples of this in our lives in formal education settings. This kind of playfulness for me is always deeply serious! It puts me in mind of my work over two years with a group of lecturers at the University of Glasgow (Walker 2001). Playfulness was central to the way in which we constructed our collaboration. We played with metaphors of dance; we watched the Australian film *Strictly Ballroom* and laughingly drew parallels with our teaching and our attempts to wrest the hope of 'doing one's own steps' from the dictates of managerialism and its performance indicators; we followed Paolo Freire's injunction that 'first we eat and then we work'! We had some serious fun! We tried to work for justice in our teaching and more justice in the university. Iris Marion Young neatly locates 'play' in the context of self-development as a process of justice, but reminds us also that just institutions are important to provide the educational conditions for people to learn, to play, to communicate, to imagine and to feel.

We need action on multiple fronts, all at the same time! We need a three-dimensional diagram that shows the importance of individual flourishing, of each of our individual actions to advance justice, of our collaborations with others, in institutions that support justice, towards societies that are more, rather than less, just. Because the last two often seem (are) so hard to do much about through our work in schools and universities, I think we run the risk of retreating into our individual actions, which, however important, are instances rather than patterns of change. At the same time, perhaps all we can do is ask: what can I do from where I am? The alternative seems to be to do nothing or not to hope, and in doing nothing and succumbing to hopelessness, effectively retreat from justice.

The struggle for social justice is hard work, but only through doing justice can we make justice. 'We make the road by walking,' wrote the Spanish poet Antonio Machado. Echoing him, Paolo Freire says, 'There is no way to transformation, transformation is the way.'

Notes

1 He made this remark in a keynote lecture at the 1989 Changing Identities conference in London, organized by Lawrence and Wishart publishers. See Rutherford (1990).
2 See also Chapter 5.

9 Room for action: creating public spaces

Introduction

For people to get political they need room to plan joint, public action. That is, they need room to discuss their views and plan joint actions. The significant words here are 'plan' and 'joint'. Action together, joint action, is 'our action', not 'my action'. A 'we', not an 'I', is responsible for it.[1]

This room, this space, is, precisely, what is termed 'public space' in some political philosophy. However, the phrase 'public space' is also used to refer to other spaces, especially the kind to which all citizens have legal access. In order to distinguish the kind of 'public space' I am discussing from any other kind, I will call it 'political-public space'. It is characterized by the following three criteria. First, the term refers both to space understood as a physical location, measurable in square metres, and to something more virtual, even meta-phorical. Cyberspace is the most obvious example of the latter, but political-public space is just as likely to be bound together by a mix of telephoning, letters and occasional face-to-face meetings as by e-mail or chat-rooms. Second, it is a space in which people are in social interaction with each other, usually by talking. Thus, people come together to argue, agree, discuss and decide what to do – so neither a cinema audience nor a mass rally nor an e-mail petition would count as a political-public space (though each might become one). Third, as actions are decided, the space becomes better defined *as* a space by the web of relations that is a result of a joint action, and that then helps to create the next one (Arendt 1958). This is a web of relations in which 'who' as well as 'what' a person is matters. (That is, the individual person, Morwenna Griffiths, matters in such a space, as does whatever reason she is there: as a woman, a concerned citizen, a professor of education and so on. See Chapter 2.) So this is a space where people respect each other and, through communi-cation with each other, help to develop the kinds of people they will all become.

Political-public spaces and room for action

The political-public spaces that I am talking about have their origins in the human desire for justice. The same desire keeps the space open. This desire is something that is found in the youngest of children. 'It's not fair!' is a familiar cry. Even if the sentiment is not expressed in words, it is deeply felt. Adults vividly remember those times in their childhood when they were treated unfairly. Young people between childhood and adulthood crave respect, and see that it must be reciprocal (even if many of their actions seem designed to test the limits of reciprocity). I am sure that a desire for justice helped to fuel my own wish to be a teacher, to continue being a teacher, to educate teachers and to carry out educational research. I still mind passionately when I, or other people, are treated unfairly, and without respect.

We all struggle as individuals to realize our values. But as I have struggled for justice, for myself and for others, I have found (as have others before me) that the struggle is not only for values, but also for individual survival. Without survival, there is no one to keep alive the struggle. This why I still like the epigraph I used in my book *The Web of Identity*, which asserts the inevitability of compromise (Spivak 1990: 101): 'Given our historical positions we have to learn to negotiate with the structures of violence, rather than taking the impossible elitist position of turning our backs on everything.'

Justice is to be got, I have found, by ducking and weaving. A salesman for deaf loops once memorably described this attitude to me as 'I cheat, but I cheat fair.' The difficulty, of course, is how to keep a clear understanding of exactly what is fair. Ducking and weaving can become an end in itself; it can degenerate into a game of mere survival. I keep in mind the heroine of Brecht's play *Mother Courage*. She lives out her values of protecting her children. To do that she needs to survive – to duck and weave – on the battlefields of the Thirty Years War. She makes a precarious living selling food and clothing. But her actions as an individual have limited use. Brecht's play argues a lack of options for her, as long as she tries to deal with the situation on her own. She can plot, argue and curse as much as she likes, but in the end her survival dictates the terms of her existence. She does not have the option of joining in as a general or as a politician. That is, she does not have the option of being one of the main agents influencing events. In the end, all three of her children get caught up in the war, and all three lose their lives. Their tragic and pointless fate is a demonstration of the limited extent of what can be achieved by an individual merely responding to events, even with cunning, and even with very limited aims.

The desire for justice is not merely an individual taste or whim. It is shared by others. The shared agreement is necessary to bring about improvements in justice. To continue the story of the salesman of deaf loops: I was in strong agreement with his proposal to 'cheat fair', and so was the Departmental

Administrator. We both colluded with his action, to the benefit of those members of our department who were hard of hearing. In the same way, the play *Mother Courage* would not work dramatically if the audience did not share many of Brecht's views about justice. No doubt, some of the audience (like me) are encouraged to consider his views, and, possibly, even to act differently as a result. Sometimes individuals are led to take action for justice through coming to understand how other people experience unfairness.

A shared desire for justice is necessary to bring about improvements. However, it is not sufficient on its own. The actions of a single person can bring about changes for the better, but – despite what our story books told us about fairy tale heroines and heroes – permanent and significant change is more likely to be achieved by people acting together: that is, by joint, political action.[2] (See also Chapter 8.) But if there is to be joint action, there needs to be agreement about what is unfair and what constitutes respect. There needs to be some agreement about what to do and how to do it. In short, there need to be shared perspectives in order to develop agreed strategies for joint political action. This is why conversation is needed. All of this requires a space in which such discussion can take place. It is this space that I am calling a political-public space.

It is all very well advocating that people make use of a political-public space in order to get political, but how they are to do that is far from clear. The question looks very different from the perspective of those who easily become generals and politicians and the rest of us who do not: women, black people, the poor, the working classes, migrants, asylum seekers, people who struggle with disabilities, people holding unpopular religious beliefs. There are a lot of us. Metaphors of glass ceilings and glass barriers express our frustration. Other metaphors express more hope that the dispossessed are able to organize to good effect, sometimes in secret. Consider, for instance, metaphors of rhizomes or of border skirmishes (see Chapter 8). I come back to metaphor later in this chapter.

Different positioning in relation to society must affect views about how to influence it. The orthodox position of liberalism is that the individual must be subjugated to the laws of the state, and that this subjugation confers specific rights, including traditional liberal concepts such as the freedom of association and freedom of speech, and the right to sufficient education to enable a citizen to function as a member of the participatory democracy. Mother Courage had all those, but she was unable to influence events. She needed to find or to create a political-public space in which she could exercise those rights to some effect.

Understanding political-public spaces

The argument so far implies that there is more than just one political-public space. I am suggesting that there are many such spaces where the dispossessed and the marginal can come together to get political. In saying this, I am going against much liberal and orthodox philosophy, which assumes a single 'public' that is open to all. The power of this view stems from the metaphor of the public square, which is contrasted with the private spaces of the houses where citizens live. (Arendt describes this very clearly in *The Human Condition*.) In what follows, I consider how political-public space has been understood (a) in terms of the distinction between private and public and (b) in terms of the metaphor of the public square.

The intention is to rethink how political-public spaces are to be understood, so as to rethink how to educate democrats, and how to deepen and strengthen democracy. Therefore, in the rest of this chapter I am particularly interested in the spaces where women, working-class people, migrants, black and Asian people and any other group under-represented among the generals and policy makers can articulate and plan joint actions.

Public and private

The concept of 'political-public space' takes much of its meaning from the kind of distinction that is drawn between public and private space, and what is understood by the two spaces so created. In particular, liberal political theory draws a sharp distinction between the two (Rawls 1971; Benhabib 1992).[3] This sharp distinction is a mistake, as can be seen from everyday experiences of trying to take joint actions. It is a common experience that there are a number of spaces that are political-public in the sense that they are spaces where individuals meet to act collectively as a result of discussion with each other. Yet these spaces are not equally open to all: they are neither quite private nor quite public.

The school is a familiar and instructive example of public and private spaces. Consider any school in relation to home and work. School is often thought of as a public place, a place of public encounters and discussion, in contrast to the privacy of the home. On the other hand, it is also thought of as a place where children are protected from the public world, the world of work, into which they are to be inducted. Similarly, a school is not the place to encounter educational policy makers and their discussions in the public space of democratic decision-making. (The school's discussions are not open to the policy makers either.) The response to this observation is likely to be that political-public space is most helpfully pictured as a set of concentric circles in which the outer one is the most public (the world at large) and the central one (a person's intimate circle) is the most private. The dichotomy can be placed where it is needed for a particular purpose. The problem with this is that the 'outer' circles are not necessarily public in relation to the 'inner' circles. Workplaces can be described as private in relation to the more public space of a school. In many workplaces, it is easy to identify the insiders and the outsiders; in contrast, the boundaries of a school community are very difficult to draw.

Then again, the circles in which policy makers come to their conclusions rarely include teachers. They attend different conferences, are members of different committees and read different working documents. Ask any teacher trying to discover what is going on in the Ministry.

Metaphors

The distinction between private and public draws some of its strength from the metaphor on which it was based: the forum or agora of ancient city-states. This narrowly physical conception of political-public space is no longer adequate. It is supposed that the debates of Athens or Rome were carried out by people who came together into a single space in which any citizen could have his (it was always 'his') voice heard. It may seem strange to have to remark that cities are plainly more complicated now. They are also bigger. The notion of the agora grows more dangerously inadequate as society moves ever further from being describable as (a) small warring city-states (b) run by exclusive elites of free men who (c) are culturally homogeneous and (d) communicate face-to-face, in person.

For these reasons, there is no analogy to 'the agora' in a modern nation state or city, or even in one part of it, such as a Local Education Authority (let alone in international entities such the European Union or the English-speaking world). The 'political-public', even at its most inclusive, cannot be a single political-public space even if everyone has formal access to some venue. For instance, we do not all read the same papers. We do not visit the same websites – and could not. (They crash!) Yet the model of 'a political-public space' persists as though there were – or should be – a place in which voices could be heard, and as if everyone could hear them and respond.

Why should a metaphor be so powerful? As Maxine Greene says (Greene and Griffiths 2002: 85)

> A metaphor is what it does. A metaphor, because of the way it brings together things that are unlike, re-orients consciousness, which customarily connects things that are like. Poetry, obviously, is made of metaphors. I keep asking teachers to think more metaphorically, not so straight ahead.

Thinking metaphorically can reorient consciousness but, equally, thinking with old, frozen metaphors can keep consciousness fixed in unhelpful directions. If a metaphor is something that frames ways of understanding, then perhaps some frames open up your world, make you look again, look differently. They invite you to try new frames of your own. Other frames constrict your world. They close it down, discouraging the use of any other frames. They become fixed, rigid, frozen and cloudy with age.

What if the old categorization, the old vision of 'the public', has become fixed, rigid, frozen and clouded with age? If so, there is a need to rethink, to think differently, for imaginations to be put to work. That is, perhaps metaphor can be used to dislodge metaphor, in order to rethink political-public spaces.[4] One possibility is to invent new metaphors. Earlier in this chapter, I referred to rhizomes and border skirmishes. These new metaphors are very helpful for their users. The difficulty is that even if these catch on, they are unlikely to displace the old ones for long. Old habits of language die hard. Another possibility is to be creative – by playing – with the metaphors we have. The limits of such play are the limits of the imagination – and, here, the limits of time and space in this chapter.

So, leaving for the time being other possibilities, consider the possibilities of the idea of a city square.[5] We could imagine what discussions might take place among the street vendors, unremarked by the crowds of earnest (mostly male) citizens discussing the latest political scandal and gossip. Or we could wonder what their (mostly female) spouses are saying to each other in the school playgrounds or supermarkets down the road. We could think of the squares of bigger cities than Athens or Sparta: London, Nottingham, Calcutta, Dar es Salaam, Quito or San Francisco, perhaps. Playfully, using and caricaturing gender, class and so on, we might notice that there are many squares in any city and that they are connected by roads. The reason why they are squares is that they are surrounded by buildings: by houses, shops, cafes and hotels, with their rooms, gardens and garden fences. So, to extend this metaphor of the agora and the spaces in between, what about talking of pavements and gardens. What if we notice that the conjunction of 'private and public' with 'city squares' means that women are metaphorically excluded from political-public life, as the men walk in the squares, while the women take domestic responsibilities. But what about all those women talking on the pavement or over the garden fence, for instance? Or minding the children? And I suppose the men in the agora come home from time to time. They are very likely to come home for their dinners. So there is the opportunity for ideas to travel both ways. Even if, to continue describing this self-consciously stereotypical – mimetic – scenario, the men (mostly) do not stay long or actually plan, buy, cook, set out, fetch or clear away the dishes, women's political talk continues as they do the chores. Or perhaps this is an affluent household serviced by nannies, au pairs, gardeners and dog walkers. What spaces might they find within the household and what might they be planning? Meanwhile, what of people who are physically disabled? Are they confined to one location, or has the city thought to make it easy for them to join in its political life? How can they find any space at all to talk to each other and to decide how to express their wishes in action? The metaphor could stretch further, but the point is made: there are other spaces beside the main square where action can be planned and taken.

Rethinking political-public spaces

A richer understanding of political-public spaces is suggested by the critique made in the previous two sections. It includes a range of perspectives on such spaces, so it is now possible not only to include, but also to go beyond, traditional understanding, rooted as it is in a limited, blinkered view of how joint political actions become possible.

The view that has emerged preserves the distinction between private and public spaces. (In this it departs from theories that elide the distinction, such as Foucauldian or communitarian frameworks.) However, the distinction is not the traditional liberal one. Nor is it Arendt's, though her philosophy has been influential in the critique of the liberal view. Arendt usefully distinguishes the intimate from the public. An intimate space is one formed through relationships of friendship and love, and is held together by those relationships. Political-public spaces, spaces where joint action can be planned and carried out, are also held together by relationship, but they are relationships formed through discussions and joint action. Political-public spaces, as was pointed out earlier, may be closed to some people but open to others, precisely in order that things may get done. So a space is political-public in that it is open to other people on the grounds of their contribution to action. On the other hand, those spaces are private in the sense that they are not open to non-members. Such a space can be seen to be private, in that if it is subject to the gaze of outsiders, communications between its members will change. Therefore, intimate spaces are always private, some political-public spaces are not, but most are. (It is probably necessary to distinguish between joint action, relationship and conforming to law. No space is private in the sense that the law does not apply there.) To return to the examples earlier, communications in a workplace, a school or a government department would all alter significantly if open to observation. However, some political-public spaces of all these institutions are open some of the time.

Political-public spaces can open up within and between other spaces. Consider the alliances that form within a school and beyond it. Consider how women, gay/lesbian educators, black teachers and working-class people make links and forge understandings across the divides of institution, role and status. Think of how Ian and other teachers in his school made links outside it, with the secondary school careers advisor, and then took joint action (Chapter 1). Think of how Anne learnt by reaching out to people offering joint political action for peace, for feminism (Chapter 2).

The number and complexity of possible political-public spaces is daunting. It is all too likely that potential spaces are used for talking but little else. For social justice to take hold there needs to be more. If it is better understood how interactions between spaces could work, then there is a chance that more people would make use of their opportunities to take joint action for justice. If it seems that all decisions are taken regardless of the efforts of ordinary people to affect them, they are unlikely to try. The critique gives a lead as to how different political-public spaces might relate to each other.

The fanciful scenario of the public square and the houses in between suggests that there are (at least) four kinds of interactions. There are those that take place in the square, close to the people who make the decisions. Then there are those that take place elsewhere but that have connections with the people in the square, including some of those that make decisions. There are those interactions that must take place in secret, without anyone in the square knowing. Finally, there are those that hardly happen at all, for lack of a meeting place. All of these have their analogues in real political actions. Walker (1998) describes the influence on nineteenth-century education policy of some Victorian women who met and planned joint actions, while appearing to be staying respectably at home. They were mostly middle-class women who built on knowledge gained through their menfolk – and sometimes in cooperation with them – to work out ways of gaining access to the structures of government. Suffragettes, in contrast, used similar spaces to plot more subversive acts, and many of these meetings had to be secret from any government surveillance. Of course, it is not only women who have needed to find other spaces to plot liberation. There are also men who dare not walk in the agora: Ronald Fraser shows how important barbers' shops were for working-class men in pre-war Spanish villages (Fraser 1972).[6] The bazaar was an essential factor in the overthrow of the Shah in Iran. In South Africa, under apartheid, women's organizations, meeting in private homes, were a source of empowerment for their members, but were working for the benefit of all black people, not just women (Mofokeng 1991).[7] The point about such political-public spaces is that they are invisible to authority, while allowing for joint action to be initiated and then carried out. There are, of course, too many examples of groups that have found no spaces in which to articulate their projects and wishes. Think of the children in failing schools, think of single homeless men and so on (see Chapter 6).

Creating democracy, creating democrats

The consideration of political-public spaces suggests ways in which education and its institutions play a part (or don't) in creating democracy, and in creating democrats. I want to use two of the stories in this book as examples: Rita (whose story is in Chapter 2) and Eulalee (whose story is in Chapter 4). Rita came to her education refusing to compromise her self-respect or her values. If she had been born the son of rich and influential parents, she might have got away with it. Instead, she escaped with her self-respect and her values intact, but with her desire for education frustrated. Her chances to learn and to use what she learnt have been sharply curtailed. Eulalee's story contrasts with Rita's. Eulalee's chances to learn were also sharply curtailed. Like Rita, her priority was survival. However, in her case, her move to Birmingham expanded her chances again: she had the scope to thrive as part of the Harambee Organisation, and its Marcus Garvey Nursery. As described in Chapter 2 by Syble, then the headteacher of the nursery, there was a vibrant parents' group: Eulalee played a full part in it. It seems to me that Rita found herself in a position reminiscent of Mother Courage (though without such dire consequences). She had little chance of finding a space for taking joint action. Indeed, her actions had to be taken without listening and talking because, plainly, few people at school were listening to her and her community. (The English teacher was an exception.) Eulalee, on the other hand, found an environment which gave her room to grow and in which to contribute to the growth of others. Harambee Organisation in general, and the nursery in particular, were set up explicitly as a result of joint actions: she was able to be part of these. This part of her education helped her to become a democrat, contributing to 'deep democracy' (Young 2000). Any political actions that Rita has taken since have been despite, not because of, her education.

Getting real: a different education

Each chapter in Part 2 has a section called 'Getting real'. The purpose is to move from an examination of ideas in general terms – where examples are used to illuminate the theorizing – to a more practical perspective. It is also important to see what practical use can be made of the ideas in specific circumstances: for *real individuals*, with their *specific socio-political positions* (race, class, gender, sexuality and so on), in *particular educational contexts* (classrooms, schools, tertiary institutions) and *in relation to identifiable communities* (their own members, local communities, advisors, universities, national or international networks of educators). This section is not intended to give lots of tips for lessons or policies. Instead, it is intended to inspire and illuminate, by showing the ideas in action, in all their contextual specificity, enacted by real people. It is hoped that these examples will help educators to rethink what they, themselves, might do in their own contexts.

'Zone hockey', a new game for disabled youngsters

Doug Williamson has designed a number of popular and successful games for physically disabled children and for children with learning difficulties, including 'Polybat' and 'Table Cricket' (Williamson 2000). Recently, he has successfully led the design of a successful new game that is likely to be taken up by physically able children as well as by the disabled ones for whom it was originally designed (Sutton 2000). Here he describes a number of 'public spaces' (my term, not his) in which problems are identified and resolved. He describes the (physical and virtual) spaces in which collaborative groups of teachers, children and sports advisors meet for the purpose.

A problem that needed to be resolved crystallized one May evening in 1999. The occasion was the annual 'Mini-Games' at Stoke Mandeville. Physically disabled children and their teachers from across the country come together for a weekend of games and sports competitions. It began with a game of Goalball. Goalball is a game for the blind participants at the Paralympics. You have to wear blindfolds, so that means everyone is in the same class. At the Mini-Games at Stoke Mandeville, they had the option of doing Table Cricket (Williamson 2000) or they could go and do Goalball. While the organizers were doing Goalball with these severely physically handicapped youngsters, or partially physically handicapped youngsters, I thought, 'This is not right! They're doing a game designed for another disability with this disability group.' There was no dignity, and professionally I couldn't see it.

Now there's a tradition at Stoke Mandeville: once the kids are in bed on the Friday and Saturday night, all the teachers get their bottles of wine and their crisps and their cheese. They all go into the little anteroom – within earshot of the pupils' dorms – and they have a kind of annual reunion. So I went in there said, 'Right, I reckon we can do better than Goalball!' Anne Craddock (a past Special Needs Inspector), a teacher from Birmingham, who, like me, is practical, said, 'Our kids are mad on Uni-Hoc wheelchair hockey.' So I put two and two together. 'What you want,' I said, 'is a new invasion game.' So we talked it over that night – with other teachers contributing – over wine and cheese. We thought, 'Yes. Right! Go for it! By this time next year – give ourselves 12 months – we'll see what we can do!'

The National Curriculum requires children to play different categories of game, including an 'invasion game', like hockey. There are versions of hockey for physically disabled children, but none of them have proved very suitable. For instance, formal Wheelchair Hockey depends on having a large number of expensive wheelchairs – and also a number of players all of a similar ability level. Also there are plenty of ambulant children with impairments for whom wheelchair games are inappropriate, anyway. Moreover, some earlier evaluation research I had carried out with physically handicapped youngsters had pointed up the importance to them of having a game that would allow children with different levels of physical impairment to play together. Equally important for it to succeed, it should be a game that is recognized by the relevant governing body, in this case the English Hockey Association (EHA).

The 32 schools that had been involved in a 'Table Cricket competition' were invited to respond if they wished to be involved. Many of the teachers in these schools were already known to me and had worked with me on other projects. Sixteen of them responded with comments and ideas. Meanwhile, Anne Craddock had begun networking with Sue Sutton of the EHA, the West Midlands

Development Officer and the national coordinator for special needs hockey. This contact proved to be very significant for the development of the game. I was already networking about this new proposal with Ken Black of the Youth Sport Trust (YST). The YST is responsible for distributing sports equipment to schools in the form of their BT Top Sport 'sportsbags'. This contact, too, was highly significant as, by October, the YST had arranged a meeting with me to discuss the possibility of the new game being adopted.

Discussions between Anne Craddock, Sue Sutton and me resulted in the organization of a pilot competition in Birmingham in February. It was hosted by Anne Craddock from the Wilson Stuart School. Three local schools took part and one from Manchester. It was so important that the game be acceptable to the relevant governing body, the EHA, that not only Sue Sutton but also two qualified Midland League hockey umpires were invited to participate. A proficient adult user of sports wheelchairs was also there, as were critical friends from the university. Ken Black had also been invited. He has considerable experience and knowledge about 'what works' on the ground. The children and teachers also took a lively interest in how the game should be designed. As one of the children replied, when asked by my 'critical friend' how it differed from ordinary Uni-Hoc wheelchair hockey, 'We invented it'!

The collaboration occurred through comfortable human processes resulting from long-term relationships. The Mini-Games wine and cheese is one of these. The relationships are being nurtured and used at the same time. Similarly, the requests for help with developing the new game are not experienced as impositions. Instead, they are joint enterprises and they both nurture and use existing relationships. It is clear that the continuing contact between myself and the YST about games and kit for the sportsbags meant that the distinctive perspectives Ken Black brings to the game contributed to the kinds of planning, action, observation and reflection possible for it to be developed on a higher status, far beyond that of a prototype format. The same is true of the involvement of EHA in the person of Sue Sutton (Sutton 2000). This contact was a new one. An organic network must have room for new members – and if it is robust, it will have developed ways of including them. Yet mention must also be made of the way the whole process has been facilitated by contemporary technology. Thus, e-mails and the power of computers in developing support materials have enabled the different cycles to be created and close contacts maintained, which would not have been possible a few years ago. Members were involved without the challenges and pressures of geographically challenging meetings.

Answering back

Each of the chapters in Part 2 has a section called 'Answering back'. I invited seven people to 'answer back' with responses to chapters. The intention is to have more than one perspective on each of the issues in Part 2 and to keep the thinking about them in process rather than concluded. Some of the contributors have addressed their response to me directly, using the second person 'you'. Others have made a more general response using the third person.

Jon Nixon. Origins and beginnings, as though a vision were revealed to her

Do you remember the act 3 curtain of Arnold Wesker's play *Roots*? It's a play about Beatie Bryant, her working-class family and her love affair with Ronnie, a romantic intellectual from another world. It is set in rural Norfolk, but could perhaps have been set wherever – in country or city. Multiple disadvantage imposes its restricted codes. It is Saturday, the day Ronnie is to arrive. Mrs Bryant, Beatie's mother, has prepared tea and the Bryants sit around awaiting the arrival of this superior stranger. But, of course, Ronnie never arrives. Instead, a letter arrives addressed to Beatie and telling her that 'it wouldn't really work'. Beatie is left alone with her loss, with her family, with her origins. 'An awful silence ensues. Everyone looks uncomfortable,' signals Wesker's stage direction. Mrs Bryant pleads with her daughter to talk to them and, at last, Beatie says, 'I can't, mother . . . You're right, I'm like you. Stubborn, empty, wi' no tools for livin' . . . just a mass o' nothin'. Beatie is speechless.

But, then, somehow, Beatie starts to talk, at first using the terms and arguments that Ronnie gave her. But in her brave and confused anger, she begins to discover her own voice. Wesker, through his stage directions, intervenes again: 'Suddenly Beatie stops as if listening to herself. She pauses, turns with an ecstatic smile on her face.' Then Beatie speaks: 'D'you hear that? D'you hear it? Did you listen to me? I'm talking . . . I'm not quoting no more . . . Listen to me someone.' [Wesker again: As though a vision were revealed to her.] Then back to Beatie: 'It does work, it's happening to me, I can feel it's happened, I'm beginning, on my own two feet – I'm beginning . . . '

What happens in these final moments of the play is that Beatie, to employ your terminology, makes of the domestic place she finds herself in a 'political-public space'. And in so doing, almost at the last, she silences her authors: Ronnie and Wesker. She is no longer their dummy: she speaks for herself. She discovers, quite simply, that talking works; and the way it works is by creating 'civic spaces' (my old, republican terminology) within which voice and agency matter. She has not as yet, of course, found her audience or her readership, or whatever Wesker had in mind for her. But she has, irreversibly and irrevocably, turned to the world. She has achieved an albeit fragile sense of agency. But it is Wesker who, in the stage directions, has the last word: 'the murmur of the family sitting down to eat grows as Beattie's last cry is heard. Whatever she will do, they will continue to live as before. As Beatie stands alone, articulate at last – the curtain falls.'

I am preoccupied, as an educationist, with the unpredictability of these moments of turning and reaching out (moments of learning, of agency, moments of human 'flourishing'); with how reality transpires to foreclose on such moments and, how, sometimes with the best of intentions, we (the educators, the authors) may unwittingly collude in bringing the curtain down on these quick, bright moments of articulacy. To be an educationist is, in part at least, to address the question of how, within a world of incommensurable difference, ineluctable contingency and deep structural inequality, we can create the institutional conditions necessary for Beatie to stand on her own two feet.

What is at stake is the possibility of an educated citizenry: the possibility that Beatie can indeed stand on her own two feet. The odds, it has to be said, are increasingly stacked against her. It sometimes seems to Beatie that, insofar as the institutions have opened their doors to her, they have only done so to retrain and reskill her, to remould and remake her, to consumerize and commodify her. The condition of entry is the denial of her past. It is as if she were meant to live in the gaps within whatever it is that other people mean when they talk about civil society.

Beatie, as I recall her, will have none of this. She demands the right to learn and to go on learning. She demands of her teachers that they teach her, of her books that they challenge her and of her institutions that they recognize her. She insists that whatever it was that brought her to this place – her origins – is part of whatever it is that will carry her forward to new beginnings. She refuses to trade the past for the future. She insists on the right to be there on the inside and the outside of her own living.

She insists, also, on the right of association. She demands membership: the right to be in community with others, albeit others of different persuasion, different outlook, different background and different orientation. She insists on the right to imagine a new kind of community: a community based on the recognition of difference. She insists on the need for new kinds of belongingness. But she knows that she does not fully know what constitutes such belongingness. She knows too that this is part of what needs to be thought through and worked through.

Beatie knows, intuitively, her T. H. Marshall. She knows that she and others have gained civil and political rights. But she knows that the social rights that also constitute the conditions of citizenship are still in the making. And she knows that these social rights are deeply and widely contested. She knows all about the long march through the institutions and that the brave new civil society has to be built brick by brick from the bottom up. She comes to the academy (schools, colleges, universities, places of learning) in part fulfilment of her social rights, but also to think through the implications of those rights for herself and others. She comes to the academy to claim membership, for herself and others, of an educated citizenry: a citizenry that can think for itself and for others.

In doing so, Beatie lays claim to a tradition of public education whose moral and political end-point is an educated citizenry. As a member of that citizenry, Beatie discovers her capacity for leading her own life in relation to others. The civil society, as yet still emergent, of which Beatie is a member is a good society: a society envisaged by Tawney and the architects of the Welfare State as a fair society; a society tested, and temporarily fractured, by the political wrong-headedness of economic monetarism; a society now, in the twenty-first century, being reworked, albeit on the vulnerable edges, through the politics of difference and the urge towards deliberative democracy.

There is an alternative scenario. Beatie may, after all, have slipped through the gaps. The odds, as I say, are stacked against her. Luck – an undeniable factor in the lottery that constitutes life in late capitalist society – may have played against her once too often. She or her offspring – whoever and wherever they are – may have slipped into any one of the myriad poverty traps that such a society springs on us unexpectedly or otherwise. She may even have fallen from the small sorrows of positional poverty into what Pierre Bourdieu in his great, final text called 'the great sorrow': the suffering of absolute poverty; of exclusion and nonentity; of homelessness and statelessness; of complete vulnerability. We must, while envisioning the best, confront that possibility. Even so, I like to think that Beatie, as I recall her, could never quite give up hope – either for herself or for others.

On those all too frequent occasions, Morwenna, when as a socialist I lose the sense of what it is to be an educationist, I come back to Beatie – and to the civic space she made for herself within and against her origins. She reminds me, always, of why I am here and of what I came to say.

Notes

1 Consider large political demonstrations. They demonstrate the number of people who feel strongly, and that is their point. They are not 'joint action'. Of course, there must be people who decided to take action, and decided that they would organize a demonstration, hoping that people would come along. But the joint action is the organizers' rather than the crowd's.

2 Joint action does not preclude the need for heroes. On the contrary, it is as a part of wider joint understanding that individual survival is less pressing. Think of the stories of the ANC, Black Consciousness and the rest in South Africa and the tales of heroism in the Truth and Reconciliation reports.

3 In some versions this is not a unitary space. For instance, Benhabib argues that Habermasian public space could be construed as plural. Since it is constructed by discourse, 'in principle there can be as many publics as there are discourses concerning controversial norms' (Benhabib 1992: 119). She gives the example of the ' "public" sphere of the pornography debate', as distinct from the ' "public" sphere of the foreign policy debate' (*ibid.*). However, the sharp distinction between 'private' and 'public' remains.

4 Other attempts to shift the vision, to melt hard-frozen frames and to illuminate the field with regard to the relations between private, public and political have been helpful in formulating the arguments of this chapter, especially

Pateman (1988), Benhabib (1992), Williams (1993), Phillips (1995), Fraser (1997), Young (2000).

5   For instance, we could try expanding on the idea that all arenas generate an audience. So, might the arena be a theatre? A television? Does the action involve the audience directly? Or is it perhaps a sports field, where the support of the crowd is essential, but only *as* a crowd. Alternatively, instead of focusing on the arena, we could focus on discussion. What kind of space is provided by mobile phones and texting? Or by chat rooms, video conferencing and e-mail lists. What kind of space is created or made available by speaking a minority language? These other games would have led to different – though related – conclusions.

6   This book is an oral history of Manuel Cortez, whose life was shaped by the 1930s conflicts in Spain. It shows how barbers' shops were a centre for political discussion. He also relates how resulting political meetings were held in private houses. Cortez learnt his passion for justice in school, despite school: 'The first time I saw social injustice was at school. Of course it was around me all the time, it was the air we breathed. But when I saw the favouritism the schoolmaster showed the sons of the rich it made me more rebellious than ever. Despite that, I loved school' (Fraser 1972: 78).

7   After presenting an earlier version of this chapter as a seminar paper, I received this e-mail from Melanie Walker: 'In South Africa in the 80s, private homes were critical to our ability (men and women, Black and some white) to keep building civil society. Public spaces were far too dangerous in all sorts of ways (although we used them too).' The other intriguing example of this is the idea of the 'street' as linking the private and the public, and this made me think of the Black women who worked as servants in our Natal homes. There were all kinds of restrictions on having friends in their rooms, so private space was very carefully controlled. But it was also traditional for Thursday afternoons to be the 'maid's day off', so all the 'nannies' would gather on the pavement on the boundaries of the white bosses' houses, and who knows what then went on.

10 Unfinished business and the DKDK zone

A continuing story

This is not my first book about social justice. Nor is it the last word. In 1995, Carol Davies and I published a book, *In Fairness to Children*, which explored social justice in relation to the four years we spent in the early 1990s, working together in a primary school we called Riverside. Then, in 1995, I was fortunate enough to obtain a year's ESRC fellowship to work on the Fairness Project with a group of senior managers in schools (including Carol, who was a deputy head by then) and education advisors. We worked to develop a 'theoretical framework for effective practice' with regard to social justice work in schools (Griffiths 1998b, c). The basic ideas that had informed the work at Riverside were used, extended and deepened during the Fairness Project. Twelve principles for work in schools were developed. I used this framework as the basis for my next book, *Educational Research for Social Justice*, published in 1998. In that book, I proposed a working definition of social justice in general, as well as adapting the Fairness Project principles for educational researchers. By the spring of 1998, I thought I had a reasonably clear and well worked out view of social justice. However, that was about to change abruptly.

In the summer of 1998, I helped to convene a symposium on social justice in education, at the Twentieth World Congress of Philosophy. One of the contributors, Richard Smith, presented the paper 'The demand of language: the justice of the *différend*' (Smith 2001). This presentation started me thinking about social justice, all over again. Richard Smith proposed that paying attention to 'little stories' – Lyotard's *petits récits* – was a necessary part of justice, in education and elsewhere. I found this notion startling, and deeply thought provoking. I took the idea back to colleagues at my university. They, too, found the idea resonant and illuminating. We organized a national symposium to explore the idea in December 1999. The next phase in my own understanding of social justice in education was launched. This book is one result.

There are changes, but they do not completely overturn previous work (thank goodness!). What I said at an earlier phase is coherent with what I have put forward now, but what I have put forward now is fuller. It places even more emphasis on action: on social justice as dynamic, as a verb. It now includes little stories more explicitly. It includes 'recognition' as an organizing concept, as well as 'redistribution'. It is also directed more generally: principles were developed for primary teachers (Griffiths and Davies 1995), educational researchers (Griffiths 1998a) or school managers (Griffiths 1998b). The focus in this book is on educational institutions at large. It is still my view that: 'The emphasis is on uncertainty, fallibility and risky judgements made in particular material, historical circumstances' (Griffiths 1998a: 91). In other words, like all theories of social justice, it is, and must be, but one stage in a continuing story. As I explain in the next section, we are always in the DKDK zone.

The DKDK zone and QAFs

It may well be asked at this point: 'But what is the DKDK zone?' DKDK is the zone of 'don't know that you don't know'. This zone is always more difficult to deal with than anything that you simply don't know. For not knowing is something that can be dealt with. It is possible to do something about it if it seems important to do so. It is possible to learn. The DKDK zone presents far more difficulty. The clearest example is a common one: lack of recognition of one's own privilege, be it of class, race, gender, sexuality or anything else. Privilege is conferred on those who hold the favoured form of such socio-political positions, whether or not the holder is aware of it, whether or not they would prefer to be rid of it.[1]

Clearly, it is important to reduce the DKDK zone. In Chapter 4, I suggested that all of us needed to ask questions of ourselves. These should not be the familiar, non-challenging FAQs (frequently asked questions). Instead, they should be the more challenging, sometimes downright discomforting, QAFs (questions to be asked frequently). Some examples were given in Chapter 4. Actual questions will need to be formulated for particular contexts, but here are areas they need to cover.

- *About learning.* What is being learnt? (including factual knowledge, attitudes and skills). Is it meeting needs, desires and wants? Does learning include fun, love, laughter, tears, obsessions? Is there an opportunity to learn how to do 'transversal politics'?
- *About personal identity.* Is there a chance for everyone to explore and discover their identities? (By everyone, I mean both teachers and students, but mostly students). Can they do this as individuals: as poets,

dreamers, mathematicians, engineers and so on? Can they do it as members of different communities? Of the whole community?

- *About difference.* Is attention paid to all the axes of difference (including race, ethnicity, religion, gender, social class, sexuality, (dis)abilities)? Are material resources allocated fairly to all sectors? Is recognition given to all? Is there a chance to explore shifting possibilities of different identities? Is space given to explore ways of dealing with being positioned by others. Is complexity acknowledged, or are some groups becoming stereotyped, made to choose between 'parvenu' and 'pariah'? Can everyone have a say and are they being heard? Is there an opportunity to have a say, using different modes of expression?
- *About the self of the questioner.* What privilege remains as yet unacknowledged? What personal experiences have been overgeneralized? Are the expressions and perspectives of others heard? Have steps been taken to find out?
- *About evidence.* What steps have been taken to ensure that the questions have been answered well: monitoring; checking; consultation exercises? What else could be used to provide evidence?

The 'take-home message'

Throughout the book, complexity has been emphasized. Again and again, it has been stressed that strategies need to be implemented with sensitivity to context and to local conditions. However, complexity is hard to keep in mind, especially for anyone in the thick of having to make many difficult and instant decisions every day – in other words, for most people in education. Therefore, I have included this short section, which gives the 'take-home message'.

Action for social justice in education should be *for and by all people*: pupils, students, teachers, support staff, managers, headteachers, officials, governors, parents, advisors and community representatives. It applies to *all educational activities*: curriculum, management, assessment, policy-making and pastoral care. It is needed at *all levels, everywhere*: in classrooms, schools, colleges, universities, local government and central government.

Most significantly, action for social justice requires *learning what to do*. Mistakes are one way to learn. Another is to keep using QAFs to reduce the DKDK zone. Learning will be well directed if it is given 'SPACE':

S: Self-respect, for all. Build and rebuild a robust sense of self-worth. Cultivate 'attitude'.

P: Public spaces and public actions. Undertake joint actions in the political. Work with others, in a 'transversal politics'. Decide and plan what to do together.

A: Actions. Take action both individually and jointly. Notice its effects and learn from both success and failure.

C: Consultation, cooperation, collaboration. Work with others, even when not in total agreement. Attend to their points of view. Form alliances and coalitions. Make compromises.

E: Empowerment and voice. Speak *and* listen. Express yourself and listen carefully to how others express themselves. Take what you hear seriously.

The acronym SPACE is carefully chosen. Space is a recurring theme in this book, appearing, for instance, in telling phrases from the stories: Ian's 'freedom to be successful'; Anne's 'space to dream'; Eulalee's 'scope to thrive' (Chapters 1, 2, 4).

This 'take-home message' should not be read as a conclusion. It should be taken as a staging post in the ongoing process of doing something about getting more social justice in education. In order to leave the discussion unfinished, the book concludes with a dialogue intended to open up, rather than close down, further conversations about what to do.

Getting there? Kenneth Dunkwu in dialogue with Morwenna Griffiths

In this dialogue between Kenneth and Morwenna the places we talked about have been given fictitious names.

KD: I found certain chapters just hit me, in terms of 'I can see myself in that,' or 'I can draw upon examples or instances I've encountered, which, in some cases, have been similar'. Chapter 5, in particular, hit me, in terms of self-esteem. There were certain things I disagreed with.

MG: Oh good!

KD: The business about respect and valuing oneself, getting an attitude: that is interesting. You said, 'Getting an attitude and valuing it.' When I was at school, teachers would say, 'He's got an attitude.' It was deemed negative, disrespectful. Yes, great! In terms of 'getting an attitude': it is almost cool, trendy, hip. But if you've got an attitude, it is perceived quite differently. I challenge that statement. I can see where you are coming from, but it is about stereotypes as well.

MG: That is true.

KD: Unfortunately, as a black boy, and all that, in lots of schools I was labelled. I didn't want to go with that.

MG: That was about survival, wasn't it?

KD: Survival. Yes. All the way through, and even now. Obviously, now I am an adult it is more sophisticated. Also, there are the differences between 'African', like me, and 'African-Caribbean'. Although I work in the context of a black voluntary organization, there are contexts there within which I have to subsume my identity. But not at other times: not all the time. It is that insider–outsider analogy.

MG: Absolutely. Yes. People must look at you and just assume that you are Caribbean.

KD: Yes, time and time again. In training sessions I use it to deconstruct and reconstruct perceptions in different contexts. Black people are not all from Jamaica! People need to know that there are many islands in the Caribbean: Barbados, St Lucia, Trinidad and Tobago are just a few. Even when you tell them you are African, they automatically assume that you are a Nigerian. What about other African countries? Uganda? Ghana? Kenya? We are all black, although people from North Africa tend to be olive-skinned. We are all proud of our identity. People need to know that we have different values, religions, languages and cultures which can be identified from the tribal facial marks of some Africans, and their distinctive accents.

*   *   *

KD: Another thing I found interesting was what you were saying about the social significance of difference. There was a discussion about the difficulties associated with dealing with difference as if difference was always a problem. You said something about the importance of 'celebrating diversity'. Yes, wonderful! But again, I wonder, in the context of the work I am doing now, especially when I am delivering training sessions.

MG: Remind me about what kind of training you do.

KD: I do sessions for public and private sector businesses, and for schools, around cultural awareness issues. I have just done some with a voluntary sector organization in Coaltown. That was about recognizing cultural diversity within different communities. So that is why what I do fits in with some of the book quite nicely. So, celebrating diversity, acknowledging differences, but also, at the same time, understanding that differences bring, not only tensions, but also – how can I put it? – challenges within themselves. It is hard to express. What I am trying to say is, when you talk about differences I thought about the BNP [British National Party]. In my current research, I hear rumours that there soon may be an elected BNP representative in Coaltown. So there is a struggle with the discourse. For the BNP, your difficulties associated with dealing with difference don't exist. They just see skin colour. You talk about socio-political differences, but they just think of visible, inherent differences. They find that 'difficult to deal with', perhaps. So, in talk about differences, they are usually perceived quite negatively, although it is true that there is a move in the society to celebrate them. In a way I hope that that is conveyed in the work I do. Sometimes I just feel it is a battle, because people are quite scared about asylum seekers. 'Refugees coming and taking our jobs and social security.' Tension again.

MG: I was a bit worried about using the word 'celebrating', because it seems too easy.

KD: It does. Yes. 'Celebrating' reminds me a bit of the 1960s, LSD, everyone just being happy. At the same time, I can see where you are coming from, in one sense, because it is about the fear of feeling, 'It is 2002, and where are we?'

* * *

KD: With all the tensions that occur, we should be moving towards cohesion: community cohesion.

MG: 'Cohesion' is an interesting word.

KD: It came from Ted Cantle's report which talked about parallel lives, parallel existences. So all the talk now is of 'cohesion'.

MG: What is your view of 'cohesion'? And of 'parallel existences'?

KD: I think we have got to be careful. There were tensions in Oldham, Bradford and Burnley – riots that led to the Cantle Report. I think to a certain extent that one has to be flexible, because you have different generations and different communities. In the new generation, now, there is a move towards integration. There was a television programme about Bradford, and they were talking to youngsters who now want to interact with white communities, more so than before. They want to go to the same colleges and mix. I think that is important. There are dangers in self-segregation. I have seen it in Coaltown. There are Bangladeshi communities who are living very isolated, alienated existences. There is a lack of services; there is a lack of communication. English is not their first language.

MG: We saw segregation like that in Northchester, where we did some research. We found that the Local Authority did not recognize the degree of segregation in the schools. But we did some graphs of the distribution of different ethnic groups in the schools. We showed that different primary and secondary schools were polarized in terms of different ethnic groups.

KD: Northchester is a good example. I studied there. What interested me about Northchester is that I did not realize that there was a big Somali community there, because it was geographically dispersed. When I was studying in another city, a good friend of mine was Somali, and he told me. But where are they? It is the same thing with Coaltown. People do not realize that there is quite a community of Bangladeshis. It is quite small, but there are certain areas that are dedicated to particular communities.

MG: I would be frightened being a Bangladeshi living in Coaltown. It has a dreadful name for racism.

KD: Yes. It's a racist place. OK, it is an ex-coalmining community. There is a Polish community there, but it is diminishing.

MG: I didn't know there was a Polish community there.

KD: It has been there since the Second World War. A lot of them were coalminers, or worked in the factories. They used to communicate in English, but a lot of them have reverted to Polish.

MG: Who has reverted?

KD: The elders. The first settlers here. That is one of the problems of communication. When going to doctors' surgeries they can't communicate in the English language, although it has been years since the war. Things like that have really opened my eyes. It relates back nicely to the issues that came out in the book about respect and difference.

MG: What research are you doing in Coaltown?

KD: It is about the perceptions of the black and Minority Ethnic communities towards four key services: education, employment, health, and police and community safety. We are looking at the barriers to participation in, and access to, key public services in Coaltown. It is funded by the Community Support Fund. They commissioned Build, the organization I work for, to carry out the research. Obviously, here I am 'speaking in a personal capacity'.

MG: Yes! Cohesion is really difficult, isn't it, because it depends on there being differences. It implies that there are different communities which then come together.

* * *

KD: Related to difference and cohesion is another project that I am doing for another organization in Coaltown, called 'Exploring our Cultural Past, Present and Future'. The central theme of this is to provide social cohesion with a group of predominantly 16–19-year-olds, predominantly white, disaffected, working-class youths. This is explored through drama and the arts.

MG: That is what I was talking about in Chapter 6, about voice and expressing yourself in different ways isn't it?

KD: Yes, expressing yourself through the arts. Maxine Greene was talking about that, wasn't she? That is interesting. I was asked to run a workshop around a South African dance, based on a miners' dance, the gumboot dance. It fitted in quite nicely in an ex-coalmining community. There are links there, you see. It is one of the strategies I'd suggest for dealing with some of the issues that have been raised by the black and Minority Ethnic communities. I remember a Bangladeshi woman saying that the racism they encounter is not necessarily overt. It is quite subtle, especially among the youngsters. So one way of tackling it is through 'dance and performance'.

MG: That is powerful.

KD: The links are to what service providers have been saying: 'What can we do that is proactive to address the issues, here and now?' The communities are struggling to get heard too. One community has been struggling for the past 12 years to get a mosque – a place of worship. They are worshipping in a church hall at the moment!

MG: They are so articulate within their own community and yet can't get heard out of it.

KD: This is it. They have gone to the City Council, but they are still struggling to get a place of their own!

MG: It is extraordinary. It is such a little thing to do, isn't it?

KD: It is. Yet it isn't.

MG: It isn't.

KD: Every time that community goes for planning permission, some excuse is made. Oh, they are going to build a shopping centre, or they are going to build something else.

MG: Yes, subtle racism, as they were saying.

*   *   *

KD: Something else I would like to raise comes from what Nada said, about the sense of not belonging and needs not being met. I know what she means about fair play and justice. Being on the edge means a degree of exclusion, even when you are involved in the process. I am not saying that people should always pat you on the back. I just feel, when you do a piece of work, the recognition is all very flippant. It is just taken for granted.

MG: I wonder if that is institutional exclusion. I think praise is in such short supply everywhere. In fact that is one way I manage people, by praising them! And it works. It is so easy to do.

KD: It doesn't take much.

MG: I think perhaps that people who are not on the margins, but who are right in the centre, get institutional recognition, don't they?

You don't need the praise so much if everything in your workplace is telling you that you are important.

KD: That's true.

MG: You probably do not need people to come by and say, 'That was a really good job!' because you know it was. It must have been. You are the main man!

KD: I think so.

MG: Take you, for example. You are 'just' the contract researcher. You still have not even got a permanent contract.

KD: Exactly. It is just what you have always said about 'soft money'.

MG: Neither do you have the big car and all that stuff.

KD: No.

* * *

KD: Another point is from Prakash. He questions the term 'social justice'. He talks about the wishy washy nature of it, and its ambiguity. I thought that was interesting.

MG: I did too.

KD: He says that it is a catch-all phrase which does not imply any professional responsibility to make changes. I found it interesting.

MG: I did too.

KD: There are dangers associated with the words, especially in the context of what I do. There are also dangers in people's lack of insight into these issues. For me, I sometimes find it quite dangerous doing a session. I feel it is very tokenistic, whether or not they acknowledge that it is tokenistic. I sometimes feel that I prefer the action research approach, the continuation. I like to revisit issues, rather than going in once – and goodbye. It feels a bit shallow. So what he had to say about the term was pertinent.

MG: I think he is right, too.

KD: I think so.

MG: I don't know what to do about it, though.

KD: It is difficult to know what to do, because it is multifaceted.

MG: But he is right. Things can just slide under the term and get lost. A whole lot of issues slide under it. I agree with him.

KD: I do.

MG: But I don't know what to do about it, what other term to use.

* * *

KD: I also think this thing about valuing yourself is interesting – about respect, value, knowing yourself. Other people may not necessarily respect you on one level, though they value you on another. It is getting a balance within the context. For me, that is in the context of working in the black voluntary sector and also my academic side, plus my drama side. I need all those things. It is like food!

MG: I know that feeling.

KD: My greens! Yes I know they are important, but I need my sweets as well! The good things are important, but you also need some other things that aren't necessarily good for you, but they make you feel good about yourself. That is how I look at the different elements of what I step into: the drama stuff, the academic stuff, the voluntary stuff. I have a degree of reluctance when talking to people, about saying I have a PhD. It is a weird feeling. Part of it is about envy in the black community. People view you completely differently. Naturally, you can't blame them. Yet I play it down. That is part of the environment which I am in.

MG: That is really hard because you care about your academic side and should be proud of it.

KD: Yes, the so-called 'self-esteem'!

MG: That comes back to the talk about 'attitude'. You have to be yourself, but there is also survival.

KD: Self-survival.

MG: It is the most important thing.

KD: It is for me. My experiences in work, and experiences in drama, are quite powerful. I am more fully being myself when I am doing drama or performing. More so than in the work context. In the work context, I suppress part of myself. They know about it. I talk about it, but I don't go on about it.

MG: That protects you.

KD: Protection. Barrier. Shield. I think it's survival.

* * *

KD: The part about what politicians have to say was interesting. About education and Estelle Morris. As you say, it is about 'boys and under-achievement', negating other elements like diversity and environment. The same thing came through in my PhD research into school exclusion. Everyone had heard that Ofsted said that black boys were six times as likely to be excluded, and because it was 'black' and 'race' it caught the headlines in newspapers and journals. And that was it. Everything else falls by the wayside. Even when they were talking about riots in Bradford, it was the same terms. In Bradford it was the Asian community. They would not define themselves, politically, as 'black'. So that again was misleading. The rhetoric is damaging. To me, it is looking at these things in the context of the environmental effects, social class effects, behavioural effects. OK, race matters, but there are other variables as well. So politicians and the rhetoric they come out with was something that came through quite strongly for me in the book. It is just sound bites.

MG: That is exactly what I was trying to say! It is just sound bites that sound good: 'social inclusion', 'citizenship', 'everyone has a stake', etcetera, etcetera.

KD: It is all about buzzwords. I am sick of it. When are we going to address the problems? Are we just revamping the wording? It is like painting over the cracks, but not addressing the problems underneath those cracks.

MG: They need to look at the complexity of it all.

KD: It is multilayered. They need to be microscopic, focusing down, but being aware of the issues and the other factors that are associated with it. But that is not happening.

MG: I like that image. That is exactly what I think you need to do. Exactly. Focus down microscopically, but notice all the surrounding factors.

*   *   *

KD: About the significance of identity: I thought of some of the comments I have had said to me, recently, by different people in different contexts. In a drama setting recently, a woman said, 'You are a strong black male.' 'Well what have you got then?' I said to her. 'I am a strong white woman.' So that is back to seeing the stereotype before the individual. 'You have got something unique to offer,' someone said to me. 'Well, haven't you as well?' I said. 'Unique' in what sense, I want to know. 'You have got an advantage,' someone else said.

MG: What they say is true, and it is also insulting.

KD: It is, implicitly. I know I have got an advantage, but he has, as well. Don't just put it down to skin colour, because it is not necessarily an advantage, always. It depends on the context and how you use it.

MG: It is a bit alarming to think you walk through the door, and she thinks, 'Here comes a strong black male!'

KD: Exactly.

MG: 'Excuse me, this is Kenny!' It reminds me of that quote from Hannah Arendt that I use in Chapter 5: 'If a Negro in a white community is considered a Negro and nothing else . . . ' As she says, if that happens, you lose who you are. You have lost your uniqueness.

KD: Yes, it is gone. Shattered.

Note

1   I am grateful to Lis Bass for this concept. She referred to it in a workshop she ran at the SSTEP conference in 2002, where we explored the many faceted possibilities of positions of privilege (Bass 2002).

References

Arendt, H. (1958) *The Human Condition*. London and Chicago: University of Chicago Press.

Arendt, H. (1973) *The Origins of Totalitarianism*. New York and London: Harcourt Brace.

Aristotle (1980) *The Nicomachean Ethics* (trans. D. Ross; rev. J. L. Ackrill and J. O. Urmson). Oxford: Oxford University Press.

Aristotle (1995) *Politics* (trans. E. Baker; revised R. F. Stanley). Oxford: Oxford University Press.

Ball, S., Macrae, S. and Maguire, M. (2000) *Choice, Pathways, and Transitions Post-16: New Youth, New Economies in the Global City*. London: Routledge Falmer.

Barr, J. (1999) *Liberating Knowledge: Research, Feminism and Adult Education*. Leicester: NIACE.

Bass, L. (2002) Self-study and issues of privilege and race. In C. Kosnik, A. Freese and A. Samaras (eds) *Making a Difference in Teacher Education through Self-study*. Herstmonceux IV: Fourth International Conference on Self-study of Teacher Education Practices (http://educ.queensu.ca/~ar/sstep4/). Accessed August 2002.

Bastiani, J. (1989) *Working with Parents*. Windsor: NFER-Nelson.

Battersby, C. (1998) *The Phenomenal Woman*. Cambridge: Polity Press.

Beane, J. A. and Apple, M. W. (eds) (1999) *Democratic Schools: Lessons from the Chalk Face*. Buckingham: Open University Press.

Benhabib, S. (1992) *Situating the Self: Gender, Community and Postmodernism in Contemporary Ethics*. Cambridge: Polity Press.

Berge, M.-B. with Ve, H. (2000) *Action Research for Gender Equity*. Buckingham: Open University Press.

Bhatti, G. (1999) *Asian Children at Home and at School: An Ethnographic Study*. London: Routledge.

Bhatti, G. (2001) Social justice, education and inclusion. *School Field, Special Issue: Social Justice in/and Education*, **12**(3/4), 143–57.

Bhavani, K. (1988) Empowerment and social research: some comments. *Text*, **8**, 41–50.

Biddulph, M. (1997) Eased out and forced in: critical incidents in the lives of gay/bisexual men who are educators. Paper presented at the British Educational Research Association Conference, Queens University, Belfast.

Biddulph, M. (2004) Towards an understanding of gay/bisexual men who are educators. Unpublished PhD thesis, Nottingham Trent University.

Blunkett, D. (1999) Tackling social exclusion: empowering people and communities for a better future. Speech to National Centre for Social Research, 16 June (http://www.dfee.gov.uk/empowering/speech.htm). Accessed August 2002.

Borda, C. and Borda, M. (1978) *Self-esteem: A Classroom Affair. 101 Ways to Help Children Like Themselves*. San Francisco and New York: Harper and Row.

Bourdieu, P. (1977) Cultural reproduction and social reproduction. In J. Karabel and A. H. Halsey (eds) *Power and Ideology in Education*. Oxford: Oxford University Press.

Brecht, B. (1987) Questions from a worker who reads. In *Poems 1913–1956* (eds J. Willett and R. Manheim, with E. Fried). London: Methuen.

Bredo, E. (1999). Reconstructing educational psychology. In P. Murphy (ed.) *Learners, Learning and Assessment*. London: Paul Chapman.

Bridges, D. and Husbands, C. (eds) (1996) *Consorting and Collaborating in the Education Market Place*. London: Falmer.

Brown, E. (2001) Freedom for some, discipline for 'Others': justice in education or the structure of inequity? *School Field, Special Issue: Social Justice in/and Education*, **12**(3/4), 91–109.

Burns, R. B. (1979) *The Self-concept Theory: Measurement, Development and Behaviour*. London: Longman.

Cantle, T. (Chair) (2001) Community Cohesion: A Report of the Independent Review Team (http://www.homeoffice.gov.uk/reu/community_cohesion.pdf).

Castles, S. and Miller, M. J. (1998) *The Age of Migration: International Population Movements in the Modern World*, 2nd edn. Basingstoke: Macmillan.

Chetcuti, D. (2000) Making partnership work: from passive participation to active collaboration. In M. Griffiths and G. Impey (eds) *Working Partnerships: Better Research and Learning*. Nottingham: Nottingham Trent University. http://www.education.ntu.ac.uk/research/

Chetcuti, D. and Griffiths, M. (2002) The implications for student self-esteem of ordinary differences in different schools: the cases of Malta and England. *British Educational Research Journal*, **28**(4), 529–49.

Clift, R., Allard, J., Quinlan, J. and Chubbock, S. (2000) Partnerships are mortal: debunking the myth of partnership as the answer for improving education. In M. Griffiths and G. Impey (eds) *Working Partnerships: Better Research and Learning*. Nottingham: Nottingham Trent University. http://www.education.ntu.ac.uk/research/

Cockburn, C. (1998) *The Space Between Us: Negotiating Gender and National Identities in Conflict*. London: Zed Books.

Cockburn, C. and Hunter, L. (1999) Transversal politics and translating practices. *Soundings: A Journal of Politics and Culture*, **12**, 88–93.

Cooley, C. H. (1902) *Human Nature and the Social Order*. New York: Charles Scribner.

Coopersmith, S. (1967) *The Antecendents of Self-esteem*. San Francisco: Freeman.

Corden, R. (2001) Teaching reading writing links (TRAWL Project). *Reading Literacy and Language*, **35**(1), 37–40.

Crozier, G. (1998) Parents and schools: partnership or surveillance? *Journal of Education Policy*, **13**(1), 125–36.

Dadds, M. (1995) *Passionate Enquiry and School Development: A Story about Teacher Action Research*. London: Falmer.

Davies, N. (1999) Schools in crisis (three part report). *Guardian*, 14, 15, 16 September.

Dewey, J. (1916) *Democracy and Education: An Introduction to Philosophy of Education*. New York: The Free Press.

Dunkwu, K. and Griffiths, M. (2002) *Social Justice in Education: Approaches and Processes* (BERA Review of Research). Southwell: British Educational Research Association.

Emler, N. (2001) *Self-esteem: The Costs and Causes of Low Self-worth*. York: The Rowntree Foundation.

England, J. and Brown, T. (2001) Inclusion, exclusion and marginalisation. *Educational Action Research*, **9**(3), 355–70.

Fielding, M. (1996) Beyond collaboration: on the importance of community. In C. Husbands and D. Bridges (eds) *Consorting and Collaborating in the Marketplace*. London: Falmer Press.

Fielding, M. (2001) Beyond the rhetoric of student voice: new departures or new constraints in the transformation of 21st century schooling? *Forum*, **43**(2), 110.

Fielding, M. (2002) Transformative approaches to student voice: theoretical underpinnings, recalicitrant realities. *McGill Journal of Education* (Special issue on Student Engagement), Fall.

Foster, M. (1993) Self-portraits of black teachers: narratives of individual and collective struggle against racism. In D. McLauglin and W. G. Tierney (eds) *Naming Silenced Lives: Personal Narratives and the Process of Educational Change*. New York and London: Routledge.

Foster, M. (1994) The power to know one thing is never the power to know all things: notes on two studies of black American teachers. In A. Gitlin (ed.) *Power and Method: Political Activism and Educational Research*. London: Routledge.

Foucault, M. (1979) *The History of Sexuality: An Introduction*. Harmondsworth: Penguin.

Foucault, M. (1980) *Power/Knowledge: Selected Interviews and Other Writings* (ed. C. Gordon). London: Harvester Wheatsheaf.

Fraser, N. (1997) *Justice Interruptus*. New York and London: Routledge.

Fraser, R. (1972) *In Hiding: The Life of Manuel Cortez*. Harmondsworth: Penguin.

Gewirtz, S. (1998) Conceptualizing social justice in education: mapping the territory. *Journal of Education Policy*, **13**(4), 469–84.

Gewirtz, S. and Maguire, M. (2001) Social justice and education policy research: a conversation. *School Field, Special Issue: Social Justice in/and Education*, **12**(3/4), 7–18.

Gore, J. (1993) *The Struggle for Pedagogies: Critical and Feminist Discourses as Regimes of Truth*. London: Routledge.

Gore, J. (1997) On the use of empirical research for the development of a theory of pedagogy. *Cambridge Journal of Education*, **27**(2), 211–22.

Greene, M. (1988) *The Dialectic of Freedom*. New York and London: Teachers' College.

Greene, M. (1995) *Releasing the Imagination: Essays on Education, the Arts, and Social Change*. San Francisco: Jossey Bass.

Greene, M. and Griffiths, M. (2002) Feminism, philosophy and education: imagining public spaces. In N. Blake, P. Smeyers, R. Smith and P. Standish (eds) *Blackwell Guide to the Philosophy of Education*. Oxford: Blackwell.

Griffiths, M. (1990) Action research: grassroots practice or management tool? In P. Lomax (ed.) *Managing Staff Development in Schools*. Clevedon: Multilingual Matters.

Griffiths, M. (1993) Self-identity and self-esteem: achieving equality in education. *Oxford Review of Education*, **19**(3), 301–17.

Griffiths, M. (1995) *Feminisms and the Self: The Web of Identity*. London: Routledge.

Griffiths, M. (1998a) *Educational Research for Social Justice: Getting off the Fence*. Buckingham: Open University Press.

Griffiths, M. (1998b) The discourses of social justice. *British Educational Research Journal*, **24**(3), 301–16.

Griffiths, M. (1998c) Towards a theoretical framework for understanding social justice in educational practice. *Educational Philosophy and Theory*, **30**(2), 175–92.

Griffiths, M. (1999) Playing at/as being authentic. In J. Swift (ed.) *Art Education Discourses: Leaf and Seed*. Birmingham: ARTicle Press.

Griffiths, M. (2000) Collaboration and partnership in question: knowledge, politics and practice. *Journal of Education Policy (Philosophical Perspectives on Education Policy)*, **15**(4), 383–95.

Griffiths, M. (2002) 'Nothing grand': small tales and working for social justice. In J. Loughran and T. Russell (eds) *Reframing Teacher Education Practices: Exploring Meaning through Self-study*. London: Falmer Press.

Griffiths, M. and Davies, C. (1995) *In Fairness to Children: Working for Social Justice in the Primary School*. London: David Fulton.

Hadfield, M. and Haw, K. (2001) 'Voice', young people and action research. *Educational Action Research*, **9**(3), 485–99.

Hamilton, M. L. (2001) Living our contradictions: caught between our words and our actions around social justice. *School Field, Special Issue: Social Justice in/and Education*, **12**(3/4), 19–31.

Hargreaves, A. (1994) *Changing Teachers, Changing Times*. London: Cassell.

Hogan, P. (1995) *The Custody and Courtship of Experience: Western Education in Philosophical Perspective*. Blackrock: Columbia Press.

Hogan, P. (2001) Justice in education: partiality and universality in tension. *School Field, Special Issue: Social Justice in/and Education*, **12**(1/2), 7–24.

Hogg, M. A. and Abrams, D. (eds) (2001) *Inter-group Relations*. London: Taylor and Francis.

hooks, b. (1989) *Talking Back: Thinking Feminist, Thinking Black*. Boston: South End Press.

Hughes, J. (1988) The philosopher's child. In M. Griffiths and M. Whitford (eds.) *Feminist Perspectives in Philosophy*. London: Macmillan.

Hume, D. (1740) *A Treatise of Human Nature: Books Two and Three*. Glasgow: Fontana/Collins (1962 edn).

James, M. and Worrall, N. (2000) Building a reflective community: development through collaboration between a higher education institution and one school over 10 years. *Educational Action Research*, **8**(1), 93–114.

James, W. (1892) *Principles of Psychology*. New York: Henry Holt.

Johnston, M. with the Educators for Collaborative Change (1997) *Contradictions in Collaboration: New Thinking on School/University Partnerships*. New York and London: Teachers' College.

Kenway, J. (1990). Privileged girls, private schools and the culture of 'success'. In J. Kenway and S. Willis (eds) *Hearts and Minds: Self-esteem and the Schooling of Girls*. London: Falmer Press.

Kenway, J. and Willis, S. (eds) (1990) *Hearts and Minds: Self-esteem and the Schooling of Girls*. London: Falmer Press.

Kniskern, J. A. (2000) The myth of the well planned project. In M. Griffiths and G. Impey (eds) *Working Partnerships: Better Research and Learning*. Nottingham: Nottingham Trent University. http://www.education.ntu.ac.uk/research/

Laidlaw, M. (1999) In loco parentis with Sally, a matter of fairness and love (http://www.bath.ac.uk/~edsajw/values.shtml). Accessed August 2002.

Lawrence, D. (1987) *Enhancing Self-esteem in the Classroom*. London: Paul Chapman.

LeCompte, M. D. (1993) Frameworks for hearing silence: why are we telling stories when we are supposed to be doing science? In W. A. Tierney and D. McLaughlin (eds) *Naming Silenced Lives: Personal Narratives and Process of Educational Change*. New York: Routledge.

Loughran, J. and Russell, T. (2002) *Improving Teacher Education Practices through Self-study*. London: Routledge Falmer.

Lugones, M. (1989) Playfulness, 'world'-traveling and loving perception. In A. Garry and M. Pearsall (eds) *Women, Knowledge and Reality*. Boston: Unwin Hyman.

Lyotard, J.-F. (1984) *The Postmodern Condition: A Report on Knowledge* (trans. G. Bennington and B. Massuni). Manchester: Manchester University Press.

MacDonald, I. (Chair) (1990) *Murder in the Playground: The Report of the MacDonald Inquiry into Racism and Violence in Manchester Schools*. London: Longsight Press.

McTaggart, R., Henry, H. and Johnson, E. (1997) Traces of participatory action research: reciprocity among educators. *Educational Action Research*, **5**(1), 123–39.

Mahoney, P. and Zmroczek, C. (eds) (1997) *Class Matters: 'Working-class' Women's Perspectives on Social Class*. London: Taylor and Francis.

Mead, G. H. (1934) *Mind, Self, and Society*. Chicago: University of Chicago Press.

Mernissi, F. (1994) *Dreams of Trespass: Tales of a Harem Girlhood*. Reading, MA: Addison-Wesley.

Mignot, P. (2000a) Metaphor: a paradigm for practice-based research into 'career'. *British Journal of Guidance & Counselling*, **28**(4), 515–31.

Mignot, P. (2000b) 'Using visual methods in careers education and guidance. *Pastoral Care in Education*, **18**, 8–16.

Milton, J. (1667) *Paradise Lost* (ed. J. Leonard). Harmondsworth: Penguin (2000 edn).

Mofokeng, N. (1991) Gender analysis in social movements: the role of autonomous women's community based organisations. Paper presented to the Workshop on Gender Analysis and African Social Science, Dakar, Senegal, 16–20 September.

Morris, E. (2002a) Transforming secondary education: the middle years. Speech presented 21 March (http://www.dfes.gov.uk/speeches/21_03_02) Accessed August 2002.

Morris, E. (2002b) Excellence across sectors. Speech presented 16 May (http://www.dfes.gov.uk/speeches/16_05_02) Accessed August 2002.

Mouffe, C. (1993) *The Return of the Political*. London: Verso.

Nietzsche, F. (1887) *On the Genealogy of Morals* (trans. W. Kaufmann and R. J. Hollingdale). New York: Vintage (1967 edn).

Norman, K. (1992) *Thinking Voices: The Work of the National Oracy Project*. London: Hodder and Stoughton.

Nussbaum, M. (1986) *The Fragility of Goodness: Luck and Ethics in Greek Tragedy and Philosophy*. Cambridge: Cambridge University Press.

Office for National Statistics (2002) *Social Trends, 3: 2002* (eds. J. Matheson and P. Babb). London: The Stationery Office.

O'Neill, O. (1996) *Towards Justice and Virtue: A Constructive Account of Practical Reasoning*. Cambridge: Cambridge University Press.

Pateman, C. (1988) *The Sexual Contract*. Cambridge: Polity Press.

Phillips, A. (1995) *The Politics of Presence: The Political Representation of Gender, Ethnicity, and Race*. Oxford: Clarendon Press.

Plato (1941) *The Republic* (trans. and ed. F. M. Cornford). Oxford: Clarendon Press.

Pope, A. W., McHale, S. M. and Graighead W. E. (1988) *Self-esteem Enhancement with Children and Adolescents*. New York and Oxford: Pergamon.

Postlethwaite, K. and Haggarty, L. (1998) Toward effective and transferable learning in secondary school: the development of an approach based on mastery learning. *British Educational Research Journal*, **24**(3), 333–53.

Rath, J. (2000) Bounding social justice? Paper presented at Approaching Social Justice in Education, BERA seminar, Nottingham Trent University, April.

Rawls, J. (1971) *A Theory of Justice*. Oxford: Oxford University Press.

Renshaw, P. (1990). Self-esteem research and equity programs for girls: a reassessment. In J. Kenway and S. Willis (eds) *Hearts and Minds: Self-esteem and the Schooling of Girls*. London: Falmer Press.

Richardson, R. (1989) *Daring to be a Teacher*. Stoke: Trentham Books.

Roberts, R. (1995) *Self-esteem and Successful Early Learning*. London: Hodder and Stoughton.

Rogers, C. (1983) *Freedom to Learn for the 80's*. New York: Merrill Macmillan.

Rogers, C. R. and Feiburg, H. J. (1994) *Freedom to Learn*. London: Macmillan.

Runciman, W. G. (1966) *Relative Deprivation and Social Justice: A Study of Attitudes to Social Inequality in Twentieth-century England*. Harmondsworth: Pelican.

Rutherford, J. (ed.) (1990) *Identity: Community, Culture, Difference*. London: Lawrence and Wishart.

Ryle, G. (1971) *Collected Papers*. London: Hutchinson.

Said, E. (1978) *Orientalism: Western Conceptions of the Orient*. London: Penguin.

Sayed, Y., Akyeampong, K. and Ampiah, J. G. (2000) Partnership and participation in whole school development in Ghana. *Education Through Partnership*, **4**(2) 143–62.

Schon, D. (1983) *The Reflective Practitioner*. London: Temple Smith.

Schon, D. (1987) *Educating the Reflective Practitioner*. San Francisco: Jossey Bass.

Sewell, T. (1997) *Black Masculinities and Schooling: How Black Boys Survive Modern Schooling*. Stoke-on-Trent: Trentham.

Sewell, T. (2000) Facilitating teacher and pupil action: making PSE work for African Caribbean children. In M. Griffiths and G. Impey (eds) *Working Partnerships: Better Research and Learning*. Nottingham: Nottingham Trent University.

Scott Peck, M. (1987) *The Road Less Travelled*. London: Hutchinson.

Siraj-Blatchford, I. (1994) *Praxis Makes Perfect: Critical Educational Research for Social Justice*. Ticknall: Education Now Books.

Smith, R. (2001) The demand of language: the justice of the différend. *School Field, Special Issue: Social Justice in/and Education*, **12**(1/2), 43–54.

Somekh, B. (1994) Inhabiting each other's castles: towards knowledge and mutual growth through collaboration. *Educational Action Research*, **2**(3), 357–81.

Soueif, A. (2001) It provides the one window through which we can breathe. *Guardian*, 9 October (http://www.Guardian.co.uk/Archive/Article/) Accessed 8 January 2002.

Spivak, G. (1990) *The Post Colonial Critic: Interviews, Strategies, Dialogues* (ed. Sarah Harasyn). London: Routledge.

Sutton, S. (2000) Zone hockey. *Hockey Sport*, June, 12–13.

Tannen, D. (1992) *You Just Don't Understand: Women and Men in Conversation*. London: Virago.

Tannen, D. (1995) *Talking from 9 to 5: Women and Men at Work: Language, Sex and Power*. London: Virago Press.

Taylor, C. (1992) The politics of recognition. In A. Gutman (ed.) *Multiculturalism*. Princeton, NJ: Princeton University Press.

Thompson, L. and Lowson, T. (1995) *Raising Self-esteem in the Young*. Greenwood, WA: Ready-Ed Publications.

Trinh, T. M. (1992) *Framer Framed*. London: Routledge.

Tysome, T. (2002) 'Unwashed' must brush up on their social skills. *Times Higher Education Supplement*, 17 May.

Vincent, C. (1996) *Parents and Teachers: Power and Participation*. London: Falmer Press.

Walker, L. (1998) Home and away: the feminist remapping of public and private space in Victorian London. In R. Ainley (ed.) *New Frontiers of Space, Bodies and Gender*. London: Routledge.

Walker, M. (1997) Transgressing boundaries: everyday/academic discourses. In S. Hollingsworth (ed.) *International Action Research*. London: Falmer.

Walker, M. (ed.) (2001) *Reconstructing Professionalism in University Teaching: Teachers and Learners in Action*. Buckingham: Open University Press.

Walzer, M. (1983) *Spheres of Justice: A Defense of Pluralism and Equality*. Oxford: Blackwell.

Warner, M. (1994) *Managing Monsters: Six Myths of Our Time*. London: Vintage.

Wetton, N. and Cansell, P. (1993) *Feeling Good: Raising Self-esteem in the Primary School Classroom*. London: Forbes.

Whitford, M. (1991) *Luce Irigaray: Philosophy in the Feminine*. London: Routledge.

Williams, P. (1993) *The Alchemy of Race and Rights*. London: Virago.

Williamson, D. (2000) Polybat and table cricket: from adaptations to sport status. *British Journal of Teaching and Physical Education*, 31(1), 16–18.

Wilson, A. and Charlton, K. (1997) *Making Partnerships Work: A Practical Guide for the Public, Private, Voluntary and Community Sectors*. York: Joseph Rowntree.

Winter, R., Buck, A. and Sobiechowska, P. (1999) *Professional Experience and the Investigative Imagination: The ART of Reflective Writing*. London: Routledge.

Wolf, A. (2002) We are still skipping (working) class. *Times Higher Education Supplement*, 24 May.

Wolfendale, S. and Bastiani, J. (2000) *The Contribution of Parents to School Effectiveness*. London: David Fulton.

Young, I. M. (1990) *Justice and the Politics of Difference*. Princeton, NJ: Princeton University Press.

Young, I. M. (2000) *Inclusion and Democracy*. Oxford: Oxford University Press.

Young-Bruehl, E. (1982) *Hannah Arendt: For Love of the World*. New Haven, CT and London: Yale University Press.

Index

EDUCATIONAL RESEARCH FOR SOCIAL JUSTICE
GETTING OFF THE FENCE
Morwenna Griffiths

This is a book for all researchers in educational settings whose research is motivated by considerations of justice, fairness and equity. It addresses questions such researchers have to face. Will a prior political or ethical commitment bias the research? How far can the ideas of empowerment or 'giving a voice' be realized? How can researchers who research communities to which they belong deal with the ethical issues of being both insider and outsider?

The book provides a set of principles for doing educational research for social justice. These are rooted in considerations of methodology, epistemology and power relations, and provide a framework for dealing with the practical issues of collaboration, ethics, bias, empowerment, voice, uncertain knowledge and reflexivity, at all stages of research from getting started to dissemination and taking responsibility as members of the wider community of educational researchers.

Theoretical arguments and the realities of practical research are brought together and interwoven. Thus the book will be helpful to all researchers, whether they are just beginning their first project, or whether they are already highly experienced. It will be of great value to research students in designing and writing up their theses and dissertations.

Contents

176pp   0335 19859 7 (Paperback)   0335 19860 0 (Hardback)

Printed in Great Britain
by Amazon.co.uk, Ltd.,
Marston Gate.